*This book is dedicated with
deepest love and affection
to my wife, Bonnie Gray.
Her love, vulnerability, wisdom, and strength
have allowed me to
fall in love with her again and again.*

Dear John Gray ...

<u>Mars and Venus in Love</u> is a book of personal examples of relationships that work—a collection of true-life tales. You may not recognize yourself in every one, but there are bound to be several that will crystallize your own truth, showing you something about your own love story that might have been eluding you for a long time. With each story you will share the clarity and love that others like yourself have found to make love work in their lives.

These stories come directly from individuals and couples who have shared in my seminars as well as from letters to my office. Each year I receive thousands of letters, spontaneously written, telling love stories. The people who write these letters are husbands and wives or lovers or seekers-after-love; their relationships appeared to be on the verge of ruin, but they have been saved by what they discovered in my work.

MARS AND VENUS IN LOVE

Inspiring and Heartfelt Stories of Relationships That Work

JOHN GRAY, Ph.D.

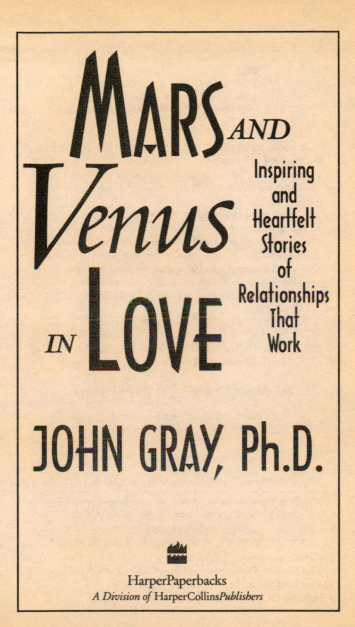

HarperPaperbacks
A Division of HarperCollinsPublishers

HarperPaperbacks
A Division of HarperCollins*Publishers*
10 East 53rd Street, New York, NY 10022-5299

ISBN 0-06-109829-9

HarperCollins®, 🔥®, and HarperPaperbacks™
are trademarks of HarperCollins Publishers, Inc.

Cover design © 1996 by Andrew M. Newman

A hardcover edition of this book was published
in 1996 by HarperCollins*Publishers.*

First HarperPaperbacks printing: December 1999

Printed in the United States of America

Visit HarperPaperbacks on the World Wide Web at
http://www.harpercollins.com

❖ 10 9 8 7 6 5 4 3 2 1

Contents

Acknowledgments

I thank my wife, Bonnie Gray, for sharing the journey of developing this book with me. I thank her for her patience and support and most of all her commitment to making sure our relationship doesn't get forgotten with the demands of writing and teaching seminars.

I thank our three daughters, Shannon, Julie, and Lauren, for their continued love and encouragement. It is wonderful to feel the support of my family for the work I do. Thank you, Lauren, for your help in writing the first chapter and the special encouraging messages you put on my computer.

I thank my agent, Patti Breitman, who first suggested that we make this book, for her continued friendship and support. I thank my international agent, Linda Michaels, for getting my books published around the world in thirty-seven different languages.

I thank Suzanne Lipsett who personally

interviewed many of the people who had written letters to gather more information. Her editorial assistance enormously improved this book and made it so much easier for me. I thank Diane Reverand for her expert feedback and editorial advice. I thank Jack McKeown for his marketing genius in having made my books available to the public. I thank the staff at HarperCollins for their responsiveness to my needs. I could not ask for a better publisher.

I thank Michael Najarian for consistently organizing and producing sellout seminars for me around the country. I thank my assistant Susie Harris for her dedicated support in organizing my office and schedule. I thank Reggie Henkart for organizing the expansion of John Gray Seminars around the world. I thank all the various organizations and promoters in various cities who have invited me to speak in their areas. I thank Bart and Merril Berens for beginning the new Mars and Venus Facilitated. I thank Rami El Batrawi at Genesis Media and Positive Response TV for making our infomercial so enormously successful.

I thank the thousands of individuals and couples who have taken the time to share with me their insights and stories of how understanding men are from Mars and women are from Venus has made a positive impact in their lives. Without their stories and participation in this project, Mars and Venus in Love would not have been written.

Introduction

As the author of *Men Are from Mars, Women Are from Venus,* I have the regular benefit of hearing inspiring success stories from individuals and couples. Practically each day, someone will recognize me and come up with a smile on his or her face thanking me for writing "that book." For years I was amazed. I knew that my seminars were transformational experiences and helped to save thousands of marriages, but I didn't realize that simply reading a book could have the same effect.

In a presentation, with thousands of people listening to me speak, I can watch an idea or a little story sail out into the crowd and see faces here and there light up, like lightbulbs. I tell a story and with hardly a pause see people around the room unmistakably and instantaneously transformed. There is a wave of recognition and a tremendous relief, followed sometimes with a burst of laughter that for most reflects the following reactions:

- He *knows* what I've been feeling. Other people must have felt that too. And here I've been feeling like I was the only one in the world who just couldn't get love right.
- The way he told about that couple's problems, it sounded so *regular*, not crazy at all. Does that mean the way our marriage has been going might actually be *normal*?
- Pheww! I'm not alone. Other people have felt that too.
- Aha, that's why that happened. Now it makes sense. I can deal with this. It's not so hopeless.

These "lightbulb" experiences are no small things. They're quick, but they aren't transitory. People's relationship problems are probably the most isolating events they experience. They are hard to define and talk about, particularly in a way that invokes compassion and understanding from our partners. When things aren't working and we don't know how to put it into words or understand what is happening, then naturally we begin to feel doubts.

In the time it takes for a single lightbulb to go on, people here and there throughout the audience are visibly transformed by one message or another—the one that makes a difference to them personally:

- *We've* gone through that! There's nothing wrong with us!
- That describes me. I'm not alone.
- *I've* always thought that love was enough, but I guess there are things we needed to know to make it work.

In my seminars, I invite individuals and couples to stand up and share examples from their own lives. The insights I relate from understanding the differences between men and women are certainly very helpful, but what crystallizes these ideas best—most quickly, dramatically, unforgettably—are their stories.

As participants begin to share personal examples of how they have used these insights to improve their relationships, everything suddenly comes together. A story shared by one that directly relates to others causes faces to shine with joy, inspiration, and relief.

Mars and Venus in Love is a book of personal examples of relationships that work—a collection of true-life tales. You may not recognize yourself in every one, but there's bound to be several that will crystallize your own truth, showing you something about your own love story that might have been eluding you for a long time. With each story you will share the clarity and love that others like yourself have found to make love work in their lives.

These stories come directly from individuals and couples who have shared in my seminars as well as from letters to my office. Each year, I receive thousands of letters, spontaneously written, telling love stories. The people who write these letters are husbands and wives or lovers or seekers-after-love; their relationships have seemed to be on the verge of ruin, but they have been saved by what they discovered in my work.

Some are readers or listeners who have loved their partners deeply, but who have—through my books, tapes, or seminars—found ways to enrich their love relationships beyond all imagination and expectation. Some are single people who had longed for love in their lives, but had never quite attained it—until they learned to identify and appreciate the differences between men and women.

Sometimes, at the end of a letter they would write, "If you think my story could help others, please feel free to use it as you wish." One day, in thinking about it, I realized that it was a very good idea. If true stories and examples could have an instantaneous and permanent transformative effect in face-to-face encounters in my seminars, why not assemble an array of them in a book?

Mars and Venus in Love covers the basic ideas presented in my books, tapes, and seminars, but in a real-life way from the *inside*, giving you the opportunity to see yourself in the stories of others and to recognize your patterns in the circumstances they describe. In psychological terms, the book gives you a safe and private opportunity to *identify* with others, but in everyday terms it shows you in a hundred different ways some comforting realities:

- that problems in love are normal,
- that there's nothing wrong with you if you have difficulties in your relationships,
- that almost everyone who tries to love has problems getting it right,
- that even big mistakes like infidelity can be forgiven and healed,
- that even when people are deeply in love, their relationships won't work if they don't recognize certain truths about men and women,
- that women and men really are different,
- and that the key to falling and staying in love is to recognize and embrace those differences.

While some of these stories are heartwarming, others are fun and humorous. What can be more satisfying than hearing of a love affair on the brink of ruin that suddenly revives and comes to life? Trying to understand how this happens is what keeps us sitting at the kitchen table long after brunch is over, pouring another cup of coffee and turning over the details of the situation—our own or somebody else's—one more time. I'm hoping that the experience of reading this book will be for you like lingering over the end of a meal, thinking about love, and suddenly lighting up—like a lightbulb!—with the realization that "Oh! That's me!" or "Look at this, honey! They're talking about us!"

1

Mars and Venus

in Love

*I*magine that men are from Mars and women are from Venus. One day, long ago, the Martians traveled in their spaceships to Venus. When they arrived it was love at first sight. Both Martians and Venusians fell madly in love, married and lived happily ever after—that is, until they decided to visit Earth . . .

At first everything was perfect, but after some time the effects of Earth's atmosphere began to take hold. Both men and women experienced "selective amnesia." They forgot they were from different planets.

Without an awareness of how they were different, the Martians began to think the Venusians needed to be fixed, while the Venusians thought the Martians needed to be improved. As they set out to "change" one another, the love they originally felt started to disappear.

Although most of the Martians and Venusians forgot they were different, some were spared. These lucky ones remembered that they were from different planets. With this special insight they continued to grow together in love.

....

Although most of the Martians and Venusians forgot they were different, some were spared. They continued to grow together in love.

....

This one realization—that men are from Mars and women are from Venus—has been the missing key for thousands of couples to experience increasing love, better communication, and lasting passion in their relationships.

Unrealistic Expectations

When we mistakenly think men and women are the same, then suddenly our relationships are filled with unrealistic expectations. Women assume men will do the things women do when they love someone. Men assume women will react the way a man would react when he loves someone. Without clear insight into the ways men and women respond differently, it is no wonder that our feelings get hurt and we end up battling with the one we love most.

> When we mistakenly think men and women
> are the same, our relationships are filled
> with unrealistic expectations.

Through understanding and remembering that men are from Mars and women are from Venus, we begin to interpret our partners' behaviors and responses in a new light. The old war between the sexes becomes instead the misunderstanding of the sexes. Something very magical takes place in our relationships; our hearts are filled with the warm glow of forgiveness and inspired by a new sense of power to realize our hopes and dreams.

Suddenly our relationships look very different. We see that our partners are struggling to be loving and in their own way doing their best. With this new insight, we are able to recognize our partners' many attempts to be loving. The clouds of confusion, frustration, and disappointment begin to clear and suddenly their actions and reactions start to make sense.

The old war between the sexes is in truth a misunderstanding of the sexes.

When we can see clearly our partners' loving intention, our relationships automatically begin to change. Instead of feeling rejected or unappreciated, we begin to see the love that not only was always there but is still there.

An Overview of Stories

With this important insight, thousands of couples have discovered how to rekindle the love in their relationships in their own unique ways. Throughout *Mars and Venus in Love* we will explore their heartfelt and inspiring stories. In their own words, we will share in their successes and learn from their mistakes.

The stories in each chapter will bring you new and crucial insights. While many of these ideas are already outlined and explained in my other books, hearing these stories will assist you in pinpointing some of your own feelings and experiences, and in some cases give you new ways of creating the relationship you want.

It is important to note that not everyone will directly relate to each of these stories—nor should you. Not everyone fits these general descriptions of how men and women are different. These stories were selected because many men and women *do* relate. As you find yourself or your partner described again and again, you will have a reference point for discussing these ideas with your friends and family and in your intimate relationship.

In chapter 2, "Men Are from Mars, Women Are from Venus," the stories explore how a deeper understanding of the ways men and women differ generates lasting love. Simply remembering that we are different from one another frees us from feeling rejected and unappreciated, and inspires a willingness to take the time necessary to understand our partners and get what we need.

The stories in chapter 3, "Men and Their Caves," illustrate how a woman's understanding of a man's healthy need to withdraw into his cave can dramatically improve a relationship. Many women have discovered that accepting a man's need to withdraw at times frees him to be a better listener. And other women find that when they accept a man's need to withdraw, he comes out more often.

In chapter 4, "Speaking Different Languages," the stories illustrate how differently men and women communicate—and how different is their understanding of why we talk at all. Both men and women use language to make points and solve problems, but women also use language to discover what they want to say, to talk out their feelings, and often to experience greater intimacy. The stories here show communication improving dramatically as men and women come to understand these differences.

Chapter 5, "The Martians Are Coming," relates stories of relationships so wounded that they were on the verge of dissolving—and yet, based on new insights into the differences between men and women, were healed and began to flourish. Here we see women and men growing in love and finding ways to get their needs met and to meet their partners' needs, where before all was confusion and resentment.

Chapter 6, "Greetings from Mars and Venus," shows the different ways in which women and men give love. Without a clear understanding of these differences, we are frustrated and disappointed in our experiences of love. The stories here serve as real-life examples showing men the importance of making a woman feel cherished, and women the value of expressing appreciation for their mates and their accomplishments.

Finally, in chapter 7, "Mars and Venus Together Forever," we look at particularly difficult problems at the heart of some marriages—abuse, addiction, deceit, and infidelity. The stories here are memorable not only for what they show about the profound effect of such problems on love, but also for their revelations of the paths away from heartbreak and toward strong, healthy, loving relationships.

In each chapter of *Mars and Venus in Love,* you will discover new ways to integrate and apply this new understanding of the differences between men and women. Each story will bring an increasing awareness of how to solve the inevitable problems and conflicts that arise not only in our intimate relationships but in all relationships.

The Magic of Sharing Stories

By hearing these relationship stories, to the extent that you can see yourself or your partner in each story, your own understanding of what makes relationships more loving will be automatically reinforced. As you focus on what makes relationships work, those qualities spontaneously become enlivened.

As you discover what may be missing in your relationship, instead of just feeling a loss, you will be inspired by new possibilities of finding fulfillment. As you begin to laugh at your own mistakes or your partner's mistakes, old resentments are released and your heart is filled with the magic of love and forgiveness.

Whether you are inspired by these success stories or simply grateful for the love and understanding you already have, sharing in the personal transformations of people like yourself—as they grow in their ability to love and respect each other—is a nourishing and enriching experience.

2

Men Are from Mars, Women Are from Venus

Men and women are different. So different that at times we could be from different planets. Remembering this single idea frees us from blaming our partners and helps us to take the necessary time to understand our partners' needs. Rather than perceiving our partners' different ways of acting and reacting as signs of weakness, or as neurotic tendencies that need to be corrected, we can begin to love and accept our partners the way they are. In each of the following stories, men and women share how helpful and reassuring it is to begin understanding the differences between men and women.

We Are Not Alone

Barbara told me this: "Roger and I are wonderfully in love today but it was not always that way. We had constantly felt a tug-of-war feeling. There were so many things that he did that bothered me. When I read *Men Are from Mars,* it was like John Gray had been following us around in our home. What we thought were our own conversations were written in his book. I had thought it was just us. To know that others were having the same experiences was immensely helpful.

> To discover that many other couples are
> having the same experiences freed us
> from blaming each other.

"To discover that many other couples are having the same experiences freed us from blaming each other. Each time there was a problem I no longer concluded that something was wrong with Roger. I didn't feel powerless to get what I wanted and most important I stopped interpreting Roger's behaviors as signs that he didn't love me."

Learning to Back Off

Nell wrote, "My husband, Stuart, is the strong silent type. He is very Martian. I could never know what he was feeling and it made me incredibly insecure. I felt I had to know. How could we ever connect if he didn't share? How could I make things better if I didn't know what was bothering him? I knew something was wrong and if he didn't talk about it, then things were only going to get worse. And sure enough, we didn't talk and things got worse.

**In my attempt to make things better,
I was making things worse.**

"I never imagined that my trying to get him to talk was making him pull away more and more. When I read about how Martians go to their caves, it helped me understand how in my attempt to make things better, I was making things worse. When I began to back off, everything changed. Stuart started being in a better mood. When he was out of his cave, he was much more attentive and interested in me. I know without this one insight we would still be at war."

Learning to Listen

Chuck said, "Learning to listen was the most important gift I received from understanding women are from Venus. I had always heard that communication was the most important element in a relationship and I thought I was a great communicator. As a matter of fact, I am a professional communicator—a radio interviewer. Why, then, was my wife so frustrated with me? Why had *she* stopped talking to me?

Every time she would talk, I would jump in with my solutions.

"I, like most men, became focused on solving the problem. Every time she would talk about what was bothering her, I would jump in with my solutions. I would try to clarify her thinking, correct her feelings, and attempt to solve her problems by offering solutions. I was attempting to solve her every problem except the one problem that she really wanted solved. She was really needing me to 'just listen.'

"She had been saying that for years, but I never really understood what she meant. I thought 'just listen' meant I should let her finish her point before I give my solution. Now I 'just listen'; I refrain from giving solutions, and suddenly she feels 'heard.'"

Doing Less and Falling in Love

Marge recounted, "When my friends kept insisting that I read John Gray's books, I resisted at first. I didn't want to hear a *man* telling me what more I should be doing to make my relationship better. Why is it that women are supposed to do all the work to make a relationship better? I was tired of doing more and I wanted my husband, Philip, to do something for a change. Although I didn't like it, I took my medicine.

"I stopped doing more for him and stopped asking him to do more for me. I dedicated the next month to doing what I liked doing, instead of focusing on changing him.

I stopped cleaning up the kitchen and after the kitchen got real messy he would start to clean it up.

"I stopped trying to get him to talk. He then started asking me questions about my day. I stopped asking him about his day. After a few weeks he started telling me about his. I stopped cleaning up the kitchen and after the kitchen got real messy he would start to clean it up. I would leave all his clothes on the floor and eventually he would pick them up. Although this was not my ideal, it was working.

> Appreciating his actions was like some secret magical love potion; immediately he was relieved and at peace.

"I practiced voicing my appreciation for whatever he did. Even though I didn't want to wait for the kitchen to become a mess before he would clean it up, I did. When he cleaned things up, I smiled and said, 'It looks really great.' Appreciating his actions was like some secret magical love potion; immediately he was relieved and at peace. I would have never imagined how much easier it could be. With this one change in my behavior, he changed. Then I started to feel in love again.

"Yes, I had to make a change, but it was not what I thought it would be. I had to let go of wanting things to be a certain way. Yes, our house is messy. Yes, he stays in his cave sometimes for days. But when he is out, we are in love and this is priceless to me. Yes, it is hard for me to hold back from doing everything and then resenting him for not helping or caring; but when I experienced that it works and that we are more in love than ever, it became much easier. It is well worth the price."

Starting Over

Judy shared, "Between the two of us we have had six marriages. This is the third for each of us. Now, in three days I'm going to be fifty-two years old. If I'm not going to have the best possible relationship after all this time and all this work, why have one at all? I'd rather be on my own than have a compromised relationship. When Ken and I married, I was forty-two, Ken was fifty-one. Adults! Grown-ups! We married to make the next level of commitment in both of our lives: by marrying, we were showing each other the level of commitment we were interested in having. And *not* having!

"Here's what led up to it:

"After fifteen years, my first marriage ended in divorce. I just had no knowledge about how to have a good relationship. My parents fought all the time and showed very little respect for each other. I thought that because I was intelligent I could do something different, but it happened all over again.

"After getting a divorce, within a year and a half I was married again. He was a nice man, but again it didn't work. At least this time I didn't stay fifteen years. Although I was confused, it was becoming really clear to me that I just didn't know how to do it.

> **When I stopped giving him helpful advice, he started to listen to me.**

"Then, Ken came into my life and everything changed. We met while attending a seminar on communication with John Gray. For the first time in my life, I started to understand men and what was happening in my relationships. I think I started to learn how to talk to men so that they would listen. When I stopped giving him helpful advice all the time, he started to listen to me. Now we've been happily married ten years and I know why.

"We *communicate,* and we know how to honor each other as different sexes. We know how those differences work. I no longer assume that it should be easy for Ken to understand me.

Sometimes I don't understand myself, so how should I expect a Martian to? When he listens and tries to understand me, I really appreciate that he tries.

I thought if he loved me, he would automatically want to connect with me through communication.

"Before Ken, I would just expect a man to listen and understand. I thought that if he loved me, then he would automatically want to connect with me through communication. I didn't know that men connect through doing.

"When Ken feels like he is doing something for me, then he starts feeling connected. Passively listening makes a man feel like he is not doing anything to help. He easily becomes bored, impatient, distracted, or uninterested. Through sharing my appreciation for Ken, he is reminded that he is helping. It not only makes him happier, but it also reminds me not to take his support for granted.

"I also don't expect myself to automatically accept and embrace all our differences. It is tough sometimes, but now I feel compassion for me for having to deal with someone so different from myself!

....

Although we are different, his way is just as
valid as mine; I don't need to be
fixed nor does he.

....

"Remembering men are from Mars and
women are from Venus helps us to respect our
differences and not try to ignore or deny them.
Ken and I went through the eighties, when men
and women were supposed to be exactly the
same. Now we know that is not right: we found
out that we weren't the same at all. But we also
learned that one was not better than the other.
Although we are different, his way is just as valid
as mine; I don't need to be fixed nor does he.

"I think there's a way men and women were
meant to be. Not just so we can make babies, but
in other ways as well. In the years gone by, we've
all gotten far away from our different natures.
Through loving Ken just the way he is, I am
brought back to loving and accepting myself. It's
taken fifty-two years and I am most grateful."

Growing Together in Love

Fred told this story. "I kept hearing the name
Mary Wright, Mary Wright. 'She's done John
Gray's work. You'd like her,' people told me. I was

becoming involved in John's seminars by then and using his work in my psychotherapy practice, so I guess it made sense to think I'd like Mary. But I wasn't interested in dating so soon after my separation—wasn't depressed, was doing fine, but just wasn't interested in dating.

"Inevitably, I met Mary at a seminar. There was dancing involved, and I danced with her, and I remember thinking, I really like this woman, but there isn't any chemistry. She's nice, attractive, intelligent, spiritual—but I didn't feel a click. It wasn't until a year and a half later that I saw her again. Mary was at a party I went to. And clearly she was the most interesting and fascinating person there. I spent a good forty-five minutes talking to her, took her number, and two weeks later called to ask her to a Billy Joel concert along with my daughters. It was a fantastic concert.

"'Mary,' I told her that night, 'I like you and I want to ask you out again. I really enjoyed being with you tonight.'

"She said, 'Me too, but I need to tell you something important. I have to go very, very slowly in relationships. My pattern has been to plunge in and get over my head before I even know it, and right now I'm working hard on not doing that again. I want you to know right at the beginning that I'm not going to be able to be physical with you.'

"'What does that mean?' I asked her. 'If I can't hold hands with you, or if we can't hug, that would be hard. But if you're talking about not being sexual or romantic right away, that's fine with me.'

"'That's it,' she said. 'You've got it.'

"We hugged good night and kind of laughed, and that was the end of our first date.

"Things happened slowly, but we established a pattern. After a few months, Mary came along with me, my daughter, and one of my daughter's friends to an amusement park. I had also been casually seeing two other women at that time, but after that trip, I saw that Mary was really the one I wanted to be with. Even so, it was four or five months before we kissed on the lips for the first time. Some time after that our relationship turned physical. A year later we were living together.

"John's work is one of the most important things that Mary and I have shared. There's a real before-and-after story: relationships before I took John's seminars and then this one with Mary after learning the work so well. For Mary, I could see how it helped her refrain from giving unsolicited advice. Being a fourth-grade teacher, she's used to telling little boys about how to live their lives, but being a typical Martian, I *hate* being told what to do. I could see that Mary learned from John to *ask* whether I was willing to hear things, and I really appreciated that. She actually did some teaching with my daughters that helped them understand me better in that way.

> I *hate* being told what to do, so when Mary would *ask* whether I was willing to hear things, I really appreciated it.

"As for me, by far the most valuable key to the success of our relationship was my learning how to listen to Mary's feelings and not invalidate them. Even though I was a therapist, John's work uncovered in me the fact that I had a lot to learn in this way. Men have been discounting women's feelings for so long that they are not even aware they are doing it. 'Sure, that might be how you feel,' they respond, 'but let's get logical, okay?' To really become as good a listener as I thought I was, I had to learn how to hear a woman's feelings without putting them down.

> Men just discount women's feelings. I had to learn how to hear a woman's feelings without putting them down.

"There's a cultural reason that explains why men put down women's feelings: males are in a kind of men's club, from the time they are little boys on up. They believe that boys are better than girls—smarter, stronger, and so forth—and they hear older men, fathers, uncles, grandfathers, and brothers put down women and women's feelings. So boys grow up without any understanding or depth of appreciation of feminine wisdom.

"Like most men, before doing John's seminars, I never realized that I had a hidden contempt for women and their thoughts and feelings. I guess I started really listening to women seriously before I met Mary, but Mary was the first woman other than my daughters with whom I was able to put this new level of listening into practice. And it isn't until a man starts to listen—I know this from my work as a psychotherapist—that women give up the anger and contempt they have for men. Until then, behind closed doors women talk about what jerks men are. But with real listening, trust develops. To Mary, my listening to her made all the difference, but it also made all the difference to me too. Mary and I began to have a sense of partnership.

"So John's work opened the way for *trust*. That's how women can relax about the cave: they *trust* that the guy will come back out. I also realized how much it meant to me to be acknowledged for the things I would do. In my previous marriage, I felt that my first wife seemed to take the things I did for granted and never seemed to appreciate them, but John's work shined the light on that particular aspect of relationships: how important appreciation is to a man. For instance, Mary would say, 'I love you,' and I certainly liked hearing that, but then she'd say, 'Honey, it really makes me feel good that you handled getting the tickets'—or 'thanks for taking out the trash' or 'I really admire how hard you try to be a good father'—and those kinds of acknowledgments go all the way in and mean even so much more to me.

"The teachings are so basic, I use them in my practice all the time. Understanding the differences between men and women results in trust, which provides a lot of safety. That's where love can flourish. And that's what happened to Mary and me. Love just flourished and grew. We were married in 1994. John and Bonnie attended our wedding."

Finding Me First and Then Us

Here's Mary's side of the story. "I'm a romance addict, or was. I had my first boyfriend at five and never stopped, was never out of a relationship, until a couple of years after my third marriage, when I was forty-two. I came from an addictive background—my mom was an alcoholic and I lost two brothers to drugs and alcohol. Once I'd been through three marriages, I realized, you know, I have my *own* addiction. I didn't do drugs and alcohol—I did marriages. Doing John's workshops helped me realize that.

> I'm a romance addict, or was. I had my first boyfriend at five and never stopped, was never out of a relationship, until a couple of years after my third marriage, when I was forty-two.

"After this major realization, I finally said to myself, I'm going to have a relationship with *me* and find out who I am. I bought my own condominium, took a trip to the Southwest on my own, and explored music to find out what *I* liked. 'This is who *I* am,' I kept saying to myself. 'This is what *I* like. This is what I don't like. This is what I won't accept. This is what I might accept.' I was falling in love again, but for the first time I was falling in love with myself.

"All during this time by myself, I kept hearing the name Fred Kleiner. People thought we'd like each other. 'I'm not interested. I'm not dating,' I'd tell them. But I kept on hearing his name. I might even have met him. And then I went to a party, and there was Fred Kleiner. He came over, started talking, and was completely delightful. He asked me for my phone number and a few weeks later called to ask me to a concert.

"On the way into the concert, I started right off with a warning. 'I want you to know, I've been married three times. I don't know how to do a relationship, but I know I'm going to do this one differently.'

"He put his arm around me, and I went on. 'I don't know if or when I'll ever be able to kiss you. I'm in totally new territory.' Kisses were my downfall. 'Can I give you a hug?' Fred asked.

"'I have no problem with a hug. But kisses— every time I kiss somebody I care about, that's when I lose it completely. That's when I get into my romance addiction and create a fantasyland.'

"'That's cool,' he said. We had a great time at the concert that night. A pattern established itself. We spent the first five and a half months going to dinner and the movies. Afterward, Fred would walk me up to my condo and we'd hug, and then we'd laugh, but I still wasn't ready for a sexual relationship. Fred was magnificent. He never pushed me; he respected me. He knew

John's work inside and out and did magical things with it.

I didn't fall desperately in love, nor did I become disappointed because my unrealistic romantic expectations were once again not met.

"Fred was the first man who took the time to listen to me. This helped me stay in touch with me. I didn't fall desperately in love, nor did I become disappointed because my unrealistic romantic expectations were once again not met. We definitely had our ups and downs but we came through it. I've learned that men need their space to work things out and that I just need to let things be. Fred has learned just to let me talk, just to listen.

"Now I can look at my romantic addiction and understand it for what it was. It was a fantasy of how I thought love *ought to* be. I was so desperate to be loved that I would become whatever the man wanted me to be and lose myself. I would become so at one with the man—my husband—that I wouldn't think about my own needs or who I was or what I needed or even what I liked. I'd just move into his life and become an appendage of him. Eventually though, I would discover that I was unhappy and I wasn't getting what I needed.

"But with Fred! We have so much fun together, and I am completely myself with him. I'm Mary Wright, I'm a teacher, and I'm Fred Kleiner's wife. I absolutely *know* I could live without Fred, could function without him, could have a completely fulfilling life without him. But I choose not to. I'm with Fred out of choice, not desperation.

"Understanding how we are different helps me to choose him every day. I don't feel like something is wrong with me. I don't have to change myself to be loved by him. He accepts my differences. He tries to validate my feelings and see the good in me. I no longer feel I have to always fulfill his every expectation to be loved.

"There's something far more romantic in being with Fred out of choice than in being with my other husbands in that sick, addictive, romantic fantasy *need* I used to have. In those days I didn't have me. Now I have Fred *and* me. Now I have us."

The Miracle of Understanding

According to Sue, "*Men Are from Mars, Women Are from Venus* was truly the answer to my prayers. I needed a miracle in my marriage. I was to the point where I thought about divorce a lot—but didn't want to do it for the sake of our children. Somehow I felt the 'answer' was on its way—and it was!

I thought about divorce a lot—but didn't want to do it for the sake of our children.

"Rich and I have been married for twenty-four years. We have five children, ages sixteen to twenty-two. During the past twenty-four years we have put so much energy and effort into raising our kids to be good, responsible adults that I think our own problems got pushed aside. Now our three daughters are in college and our two sons are almost finished with high school—so I feel our job is almost done. And we are starting to focus more on each other and on getting along.

"Our main problem in the past twenty-four years has been our lack of communication. Whenever I would say how I was feeling about a problem with the kids, Rich would get defensive and attack me with how it was my fault—usually because of my lack of discipline with them, he would say.

"He could never listen to me without trying to

'fix' me or the problem. I would always end up crying, wishing I had never even tried to talk to him. He had a bad temper that would flare up, and he'd say hurtful words to me too.

"But after reading your book with me, he understands me and his temper is better. Because of what you say about women in your book, which is exactly the way I am, for the first time ever he realizes that I am 'normal.' Now I can share my feelings and thoughts with him without him getting angry at me.

For the first time ever he realizes that I am "normal."

"In chapter 5, you say that a man needs to remember that by complaining about a problem a woman isn't necessarily blaming him; instead, she is letting go of her frustrations by talking about them. You say that women talk about their problems to feel better, whereas men go into their 'caves' to solve their problems alone. When we realized that this was what we were doing, our marriage was on its way to recovery.

"As we read each chapter, we got excited about the changes that were taking place in our lives. When I'd get home from work, Rich would actually sit down with me and ask me how my day went—and listen to me talk! This was something I needed that he had learned from your book.

"In chapter 10, when you tell about how a woman 'keeps score,' and how the little things a man does mean just as much as the big things, this rang so true with me. I was 'keeping score' all those years in my mind and didn't even realize I was doing it. And I always had a lot more 'points' than Rich, so the score was always uneven—which caused me to resent him a lot. I was always sick with the 'resentment flu.' Wow! I had built up *so* much resentment in my heart toward him that it poisoned our relationship, and one day I said to him, 'I have love for you, but I don't like you as a person anymore.' I wasn't in love with him anymore because of all the resentment in my heart.

I wasn't in love with him anymore because of all the resentment in my heart.

"It was just a few months later that we received your book as a gift from Rich's brother, Jon, who lives in California. He had heard you speak on relationships and liked what you said, so that's how we got your book in this frozen northland (it was twenty below zero this morning!).

"After reading your book, I wrote Rich a nine-page 'love letter' and put all my feelings down on paper. I learned that by writing down my negative feelings, they lose power so that positive feelings can emerge. I did the 'P.S.' response part too, that you talked about in chapter 11—writing the response to my letter that I wanted from Rich—and this is what helped me the most. This is where the healing truly began in my heart.

**His very loving apology letter started
to heal my hurt feelings.**

"When I showed Rich my letter and 'his' response, he responded with a very loving apology letter that started to help heal my hurt feelings too. We discovered new things about each other from this. I found that the best way to communicate with him was by writing love letters. Even today, if I am really upset and try to tell him my feelings, he usually blows up at me; so now I know that it's best to write them down. Without this method, I would have died from the 'resentment flu,' which was caused from getting my feelings hurt so many times when I was trying to talk to him.

"Our relationship has improved a lot in the last two years, since we read your book. Now we understand each other better. We understand why we both act the way we do. I believe that the truth in your book saved our marriage. For this I will be forever grateful. Now the score is more even at our house, as Rich does the laundry, some cooking, and helps out more with all the little things that make a big difference in a marriage relationship. We still have our ups and downs, but we are on the road to recovery and there is hope for our marriage again."

3

Men and Their Caves

Without a doubt the most important and useful information for Venusians about Martians is understanding men and their caves. The insight—that a man can love his wife but sometimes not want to spend time with her—is quite surprising for many women and generally very foreign to their nature.

When a woman is in love with her man, she looks forward to spending time together and sharing. Even if she is feeling stressed, she still looks forward to sharing the details of her day with the man she loves. For her, talking and sharing helps to sort things out and release the burdens of the day; it creates intimacy and simply makes her feel better.

For her to connect with her partner and receive his support is one of the major benefits of a relationship. It just feels good when someone who cares also understands what you go through. The more a Venusian loves a man, the more she wants to share with him.

It is very frustrating and disappointing when her beloved Martian comes home and has literally nothing to report. When she asks if something is bothering him, he says, "It's nothing." She doesn't understand that he means, "I'm in my cave for a while, I would rather not talk right now. After a while I'll be out."

**A woman mistakenly takes it personally
and feels rejected when a man pulls
away into his cave.**

Without understanding that men are from Mars, she can't help but take it personally. She assumes he must not love her if he doesn't want to share with her. Understanding and accepting a man's cave time is essential for every woman who lives with a man, or plans to one day. Although this is much harder than it sounds, these examples may make it easier.

He Still Loves Me

Janet related, "When a girlfriend is mad at me she doesn't want to talk. On Venus, not wanting to talk is the clearest and most definite sign that there is a big problem in the relationship. So when my husband, Carlos, didn't want to talk, I would begin to panic. I would worry about what I had done. Then, after feeling bad for a while, I would get mad that he was rejecting me and I hadn't done anything wrong. Then I would feel hurt.

"Put most simply, when he went to his cave, it was very difficult. When I would want to talk, and he didn't, he would either become bothered by me or just get distracted. When I said he wasn't listening, it just made things worse and we would argue.

"Even though he would tell me nothing was wrong, I didn't believe him. I knew that whenever I didn't want to talk, something was wrong. Reading about the cave has made such a difference. It was a relief to know he still loved me. I couldn't accept that he loved me until I learned that it was not just him, that all Martians regularly go to their caves.

> I couldn't accept that he loved me until I
> learned that it was not just him, that all
> Martians regularly go to their caves.

"I was so relieved to discover it didn't mean he loved me less. Before this insight I had felt he didn't love me as much as I loved him. Now I just wait for him to come out of his cave and then I talk. He is usually much more interested. I am so grateful to finally understand my Martian."

It's Not My Fault

Anna shared, "When he was in his cave I always thought I had done something wrong; I thought it was my fault. This made me feel guilty and then I would try to be more pleasing to him. I did everything I could think of. I would try to make the house really clean, I would make his favorite meals, I would not ask for anything more, and then—when he would still go to his cave—I would become very resentful.

> When he was in his cave I always thought
> I had done something wrong; I
> thought it was my fault.

"Nothing I did seemed to make a difference. After a while I started to believe that it was my fault that I married the wrong man. Now I am relieved to know I just married a Martian. Instead of doing more for him when he is in his cave, I just ignore him and do things for me. I am still surprised that he is not angry with me. He likes when I give him lots of space. I would prefer to be closer more of the time but this sure beats resenting him.

"It gives me hope to know that as a man matures he gradually needs less time in his cave and as a woman matures she becomes more autonomous and less needy at those times when he is in his cave. I think that the less it bothers me that he is in his cave, the less time he spends in there."

The less it bothers me that he is in his cave, the less time he spends in there.

Venusians Need Caves Too!

Laura had a terrific insight: "Learning to simply accept my partner's need to spend time in his cave has not only created peace in our relationship but it has taught me something very important about myself. Giving him permission to take care of himself at those times gave me permission to take care of myself as well. When I come home from work, instead of jumping into my domestic duties or trying to be the loving wife, I take some time for myself. I figured that if he can do so, then I can too.

> Giving him permission to take care of himself gave me permission to take care of myself as well.

"Although my cave looks different from his, it is still time for me and not for anyone else. While he reads a magazine or watches TV, I like to go for a walk or work in my garden. That is my cave. Ironically, by learning to embrace his cave time, I started giving myself what I had always needed but had never given to myself.

"P.S.: I am still a Venusian, however; when we are out of the cave, I like to take the time to talk and now he listens."

I Need More Space

Carol had another point of view: "About withdrawing into the cave, it's funny. It's me that does that more than Jack. I need much more privacy than he does. While he was married for all those years, I spent some of my happiest years alone. I seem to need more space. I do think he resents that I go into my cave sometimes, but I've learned to reassure him that I'm going to come back out. It's not really an issue as long as I remember to appreciate the things he does for me. He knows that if I am not attentive to him and his needs because I am in my cave, it is certainly not that I don't appreciate all that he gives me."

I'll Be Back

Janie described how she and her husband changed their behavior: "After reading your books, my husband, Pat, made one small change that has made a big difference in our relationship. He understands that his cave time is hard on me.

"He realized that his pulling away was hard on me. I don't mind working to let him be in his cave, as long as he realizes that it is hard and sometimes it still hurts. When I feel neglected and ignored, he doesn't use the cave as a defense or excuse. Instead he tries to listen and then plans some special time for us.

When I feel neglected and ignored, he doesn't use the cave as a defense or excuse.

"He doesn't have to give up the cave, but it is nice that he shows that he cares about my feelings. Another way he shows me that he cares is when he says, 'I just need to go for a drive. I'll be back in a little while.' This one comment—'I'll be back'— makes it much easier and I love him for it."

Coming Back from the Cave

Tom revealed his self-doubt: "I have been married thirty-six years and I always thought something was wrong with me. When I heard other men also have a cave, I burst into tears. I had thought I would never be able to really love a woman. I had always felt like such a disappointment to my wife. I would try to be caring and attentive, but inside I just didn't feel it. Nobody ever told me it was okay at those times to just go to my cave.

"Now, when I don't feel warm and loving, I

just stop trying and instead do something that I like doing. Many times I just take a nap or go to the movies with a buddy. Then next day, the spell is broken and I am back to loving my wife again. When I pull away, she doesn't feel so disappointed either. That is a relief.

If I've been in the cave for a few days, when I'm back, I do something special, like bring her flowers or clean up the kitchen.

"I am so grateful that she understands me now even though she doesn't like it very much. After I go to my cave for a while, I always make sure that when I'm back I do something special or show some affection. If I've been in the cave for a few days, I make sure to bring her flowers or clean up the kitchen when I'm back. Doing little things make a big difference and it also lets her know that I am in touch with my loving feelings again."

Having Fun with the Cave

Kyle had a clever solution: "Before taking John's workshop, I would go into my husband's cave and want to decorate it, put up pictures of myself, leave hair clips and nail polish lying around. Though I didn't know it, this was a major violation in Martianville, and Gary kept taking my nesting objects out of his cave. Why didn't he want to be surrounded with the essence of his loving wife? I wanted to know. With an understanding of the cave, I could let go and give him what he needed.

"Gary was excited to know that it was not only okay but mandatory for him to create his own space. One day I came home and heard an intense drilling noise in the back part of the house. It turned out that Gary had put a deadbolt lock on the room he had designated his cave. Now he could actually lock himself in.

Gary was excited to know that it was not only okay but mandatory for him to create his own space.

"On the outside of his door I hung a big ugly gorilla in the form of a doorbell ornament. Every time you press the button, the gorilla's red eyes light up, his mouth opens, and he makes a roaring sound. Gary threw out my nesting stuff, but he rather liked the gorilla. He and I both understood. We added fun to the cave idea and I learned not to take it personally. Gary needs his cave time. When the door is locked, I don't attempt to enter."

Accepting the Cave

Rose told how she came to understand the cave: "Before I read your book, I was doing everything wrong. When my husband went to his cave I had to follow. I thought I was doing the right thing. I thought it was my job to go in there and get him. If I didn't, then I wasn't a loving wife.

"For over twenty years I have tried everything to get into his cave. I used dynamite to get in. I was a real cave buster!

**I used dynamite to get in.
I was a real cave buster!**

"But when the smoke and dust would clear, I looked around in his cave and he still wasn't there. He was busy digging tunnels to escape me.

"Now I just let him go in there. He comes out all on his own. I've learned the hard way. Anything I do to get him out only makes things worse. When he goes to his cave, I go shopping. We are both so much happier. We are in love again."

Flying Caves

Lynette confessed, "I used to be so hurt when Chris would leave each week for his job. We could spend a wonderful romantic weekend together and then the next day he was off. I was hurt because I thought he loved his work more than me. Even before he left, I started missing him. I was sad but he was happy and excited. I just couldn't understand why he didn't want to spend more time with me.

"Learning about Martians and their need to be on their own, independent and adventurous, helped me not take it so personally when he was excited about leaving. When I learned about the cave, I realized that flying off in airplanes was his way of going to his cave: a flying one. Now, when he is excited about leaving, I realize it is not that he is excited about leaving me; it is that he is excited about going off on an adventure.

"Instead of resenting it when he leaves for a few days, I appreciate that he gets his cave time so that when he is with me, he can be fully here."

Changing Expectations

Krista explained, "Understanding men and their caves changed all my expectations. When he seems distant and aloof I don't panic. It is temporary. I just say 'cancel' to all my automatic responses like, It's my fault, I did something wrong, he doesn't love me, I failed him in some way, he doesn't care for me as much as he used to.

"Now I know he's just doing his Martian thing. It has nothing to do with me. It just means that he has little love to share and that he is taking the time he needs to feel better about himself. He is taking the time he needs for himself so that he will be able to give me the love and attention that I need."

The Man of My Dreams

Lucy recounted, "On May 30, 1991, I met the man of my dreams. His name is Peter Clark. We married a year later, and are now raising his three sons. I am in love with him still. Each morning I am awakened by a man who reaches out for me before he starts his day. And at the end of each hectic day, we are happy just to be in each other's arms again. He understands my Venusian needs and I have learned about his Martian needs. Life is worth living when Venus and Mars are in love.

"But 'bliss' takes work. And, sometimes, skill.

"Peter has many special skills that make me a happy Venusian. For instance, my husband listens to *every word I say!* I know, you couldn't possibly believe me . . . it is so un-Martian! Yet when I ramble on for minutes, half hours, even hours, he listens patiently as I relive and replay every thought and emotion and detail that I went through. He doesn't fidget or get distracted or make me feel that I am imposing on him. He just listens to the whole thing. He doesn't even offer advice or insight. Peter has been a listening Martian since day one of our relationship. So, of course, *I had to fall in love with him!*

"Learning about his cave has been an enormous help in our relationship. It helps make sense of why sometimes he is so attentive and then at other times he withdraws for days. Before, I used to feel that for some mysterious reason he was rejecting me.

"One evening when he had been withdrawn for several days, I put my arms around his neck and asked, 'Honey, are you in your cave?'

"'Oh, I guess I am,' he replied.

"'It's getting lonely out here,' I told him.

"'Oh, I'm sorry.' And after just a moment's hesitation, he added, 'But I just want you to know that while I was in my cave, your picture was on the wall!'

"But I just want you to know that while I was in my cave, your picture was on the wall!"

"Wow! Spoken loud and clear, right to my Venusian heart! As far as I was concerned, he could go back in his cave for a week, and I'd still know our relationship was important to him."

Commitment in Action

Pam had a story that lasted thirty-five and a half years. "I wanted to share our love story because of its perspective on commitment in action. First, let me introduce myself and my husband. We have been married for thirty-eight and a half years and have five children and five grandchildren. We have had three major career changes—from teaching to owning our own electrical business to pastoring two churches. When we grew to love each other and married, in 1957, my husband had four years of college behind him and two left to go before graduation (he had changed his major). He then went on after his degree to obtain a master's, doctorate, and second bachelor's degree.

"Those early years were marked every two years by the birth of another baby. Still, we remained very much in love, with lots of chemistry and passion. By today's standard we married too young—twenty and twenty-two and a half. But we understood the full meaning of the word 'commitment,' and both agreed it meant a lifetime, no matter what. That commitment has helped us to make peace with our differences.

**Commitment has helped us to make
peace with our differences.**

"We learned after a few years of marriage, to our surprise, that we were totally opposite. He is Mr. Clean and I'm the queen of clutter. He likes to finish everything; I'm open-ended. He has to be alone to charge his battery; I hate to be alone more than an hour or so.

"Although there was conflict, our commitment to make our marriage work helped us to find a solution. The solution always required once again learning to accept and allow the other person to be himself.

"It gives me comfort to understand that when

my husband goes into his cave to figure things out, he is being a man, that his retreat has nothing to do with me and that he will be back. We have even joked about him wearing a sign stating, 'In cave/out of cave.'

"Once I unknowingly ventured uninvited into his cave and attempted to help him solve a computer problem. Oh, what a mistake! At least I was able to realize why he was so annoyed.

I have gradually learned to accept that he has to be alone to charge his battery, while I hate to be alone more than an hour or so.

"Learning to accept and allow Warren to be himself is a growth process. Differences are not wrong; they keep the passion alive. Warren's need to pull away does not mean he is not committed to our relationship. Our love for each other has grown, blossomed, and ripened.

"We have weathered the challenges of education, three major job changes, five children, male and female differences, personality and temperament differences, and now, at present, aging parents . . . only to pay tribute to the word and process of continual commitment to each other, our love, and making it work.

"It takes more than *love* to make our marriage work; it takes commitment, education, skills, insight, and tools. We supplied the love and commitment, and John Gray supplied the education, communication skills, insights, and tools."

He Wouldn't Call

Josie learned how to deal with a troubling problem: "Most of the time, when Harold was out of town working, he wouldn't call. I couldn't believe that he didn't want to talk with me. I would feel so hurt that when he came home I wouldn't talk to him. I just couldn't open up after being ignored this way.

"This was even more confusing for him. He said, 'If you miss me so much when I am away, then why do you reject me when I get home. It seems you would be happy to see me because now we can be together.' His 'logical' argument didn't go over with me.

"After reading *Men Are from Mars,* I was able to look at it differently. Before I would take it personally, but now I know it's not that he doesn't want to talk to me but that he is just focused on his work. Even though he doesn't call, he does look forward to coming home and being with me.

"I told him it was okay if he didn't call but that when he did call I would really appreciate it. Now sometimes he calls and sometimes he doesn't. It is no longer a sore spot. When he does call, though, I don't just take it for granted—I make sure to let him know how glad I am."

Controlling Anger

Carolynn described improved communication with her husband. "I am twenty-nine years old and currently a student full-time. My husband, Frank, is thirty-six. Since reading *Men Are from Mars,* our way of communicating has changed. Let's go back to January 1994, when we'd been together for ten years.

"Frank and I truly loved each other all those years, but we had some serious problems. He was a very short-tempered, angry individual, and I was extremely critical and demanding. In January 1994, we experienced the biggest, meanest, and, yes, most violent fight of our relationship. We separated, knowing that we loved each other very much but were just not 'doing it right'—communicating and sharing. Frank joined an 'anger-management group' and I started seeing a therapist. Eight months later, we were happy to say that the dysfunctional part of our relationship had disappeared. Frank was able to use different techniques—for example, time-outs, physical release methods, and so on—to control his anger, and I learned that my judging and critical comments were my own insecurities surfacing.

We experienced the biggest, meanest, and most violent fight of our relationship.

"With the big obstacles out of the way, we thought our relationship would be perfect. Haha! We started having bigger problems . . . communication problems. Frank would constantly go into his cave, and I would become resentful and proceed to pull him out. These very serious problems started making us doubt our true love for each other.

"Luckily, my therapist recommended that I read *Men Are from Mars*. Frank and I made a commitment to read a chapter together every week, but even in the first chapter we were hooked. And since that time, our lives have changed. I let him stay in his cave and know that he is doing what he needs to do so that we can talk later in a more understanding and compassionate manner. We still have arguments, but we learn and grow from them now.

"When I tend to 'go on and on,' Frank understands that I really just need to talk to figure out what's bothering me. He remembers that we are from different planets and doesn't try to 'fix' me. I also have learned that sometimes he will need to go into his cave. I now know that this doesn't mean he doesn't love me or that he won't come back.

"I have heeded Dr. Gray's advice, telling Frank, 'You know, I'm beginning to feel restless and resentful, so I'm going to do something for myself.' And I do; I go shopping or call a friend. This, in turn, takes the pressure off Frank. Just as Dr. Gray mentioned in one of his lectures, the more you practice daily communication techniques, the less often will the man enter his cave, and when he does go in, the less time he will spend there.

"You know, I'm beginning to feel restless and resentful, so I'm going to do something for myself."

"We still have our high-stress times. However, slowly we become better and better at handling our own emotions. Someone wise once told me, 'Carolynn, it took you and Frank ten years to build this pattern of communication. Give yourself at least half that time to learn, practice, and perfect it.' Thanks to Dr. Gray, we have learned how to do so effectively and sincerely. We truly didn't know how even to attempt good communication before. Both of us learned from our parents that when you are upset with your partner you yell, get angry, hit, and never ever make yourself vulnerable by telling your partner that you're sad or hurt.

"Thank you, Dr. Gray, for writing a book that explains to simply be nice to each other. When you are not exposed to the right way to communicate in a relationship, you simply don't know how. Now we do, and often find ourselves referring to your book."

My Mind Was Glued to the Job

Ross explained that he needed to change. "My wife, Brenda, always used to complain that I wasn't listening to her. She was right. I would try to listen but after a few minutes I went right back to thinking about projects at work. My mind was glued to the job.

"After reading *Men Are from Mars*, I realized that I didn't have a cave. When I would come home, my mind was still at the office. I needed some kind of diversion to help me let go of the pressures of work. I needed a cave-time activity.

> **I needed some kind of diversion to help me let go of the pressures of work.**

"Now when I get home I take about twenty minutes to play my keyboard or just listen to some music. It's all I need to relax and forget my deadlines. Then the next thing I do is find Brenda and see if I can help her or start a conversation. Now I can listen to her without being so distracted. She appreciates that I give her my full attention and she doesn't interrupt me when I'm in my cave."

Healthy Intimacy

Candice gained understanding: "I always dreamed that one day I would fall in love with my Prince Charming and we would grow closer as we grew old together. But in reality, I would meet one man after another, but none fit my picture. All the men I met were afraid of intimacy. We would grow close and then they would grow distant. When would I find one who didn't need years of therapy?

"I wanted a man who could open up to me and share his heart and soul. I wanted to be a team. We would always come together to share our feelings, problems, and needs. Someone who depended on me and I on him. It seemed in every relationship after a few months the man would back off in some way. When I tried to get him to talk, there was always 'nothing' to talk about or he would feel smothered.

"I was so surprised to find that these men were not afraid of intimacy, nor did they need years of therapy—they were from Mars. What a difference it has made for me! Now, when my boyfriend pulls back, I don't panic and definitely I don't ask him a bunch of questions or try to get him to talk.

Men were not afraid of intimacy, nor did
they need years of therapy—they
were from Mars.

"I am now in a beautiful relationship. Much of the time it is just what I want and at other times I just let go and trust that he will come out of his cave on his own. Much to my surprise, he does. I had always thought that the men in my life had run away from me. Through understanding men and their caves, I learned how I had been pushing them away. I am grateful to have a new model of healthy intimacy, which is achieved through a balance of alone time and together time, a loving blend of being independent and dependent—interdependence.

How Long in the Cave Is Too Long?

Sally needed signals. "I used to wonder how long in the cave is too long. Gradually I realized that there is no right amount of time. Sometimes it is weeks and other times it is just hours. What was most frustrating for me was to not know when he was out. I didn't want to be ignoring him and giving him space if he was out of the cave.

What was most frustrating for me was to not know when he was out of the cave.

"I liked your idea of having clear signals. Now, when he is out of his cave, he lets me know. He starts touching me and being affectionate. He also knows the longer he has been in the cave, the more romance I need to fully open up again to him. It is hard not to take it personally when suddenly I am being ignored. Learning to give to myself at those times not only frees him from feeling pressured, but has helped me be less needy. I clearly see that the more I can let go of needing intimacy when he pulls away, the easier it is for him to come out."

Repeating My Parents' Marriage

Mary realized she had an option. "When I married Stephen, I didn't want my marriage to look like my parents' marriage. But after a few years I found myself doing the same things my mother did.

"I am sure that she did what she did because she didn't know another way. When my dad went to his cave, Mom would nag him, complain to him, ask lots of questions, and then criticize him for pulling away. She blamed him for her unhappiness and eventually withdrew herself and stopped talking.

When my dad went to his cave,
Mom would nag him, complain to him,
ask lots of questions, and then criticize
him for pulling away.

"I promised myself that we would talk and work things out. But I still didn't understand the cave. So, when Stephen withdrew, I would try to get him to talk. Eventually I found myself nagging, complaining, and asking him lots of questions—just like Mom. I felt he was not cooperating and eventually started to blame him. I realized I had married my father and I had become my mother.

"When I read *Men Are from Mars,* I discovered that he was *not* my father, but they were both related—they were from Mars. Reading *Men Are from Mars* has given me a choice. Before I didn't really have an option, I just did what she did."

4

Speaking Different Languages

After men read my books or watch the videos of my seminars, many of them comment on one thing. For them, the most helpful insight involves discovering how women communicate for different reasons than men do. It sometimes seems that we are speaking different languages.

Women use language, just like men do, to make points and solve problems. However, they also use talking as a way of discovering what they want to say; and sometimes they talk about their feelings in order to sort things out, as a means toward eventually feeling better. At other times, women feel a need to share and express their feelings, simply as a means to get closer, to experience greater intimacy.

Men don't instinctively understand these various approaches, because men tend to use language primarily as a way of making points. When men talk about problems, they are generally looking for solutions. A man mistakenly assumes that when a woman talks about her feelings and problems his role as listener is to efficiently assist her in feeling better by offering her solutions. Like a fireman in an emergency situation, he is impatient to get to the fire and put it out as quickly as possible. When she is upset, he wants to put out the fire of her feelings by giving solutions.

When she is upset, he wants to put out the fire of her feelings by giving solutions.

Learning to listen *patiently*—and not just *passively*—is a new skill for men. Yet repeatedly men report that keeping quiet and resisting the strong tendency to interrupt a woman with solutions has dramatically improved their relationships. Their partners are much happier and appreciative. Lucky is the man who discovers that satisfying a woman's need to communicate and be heard is the most important requirement in making relationships loving and harmonious. When a man is a good listener, a woman can repeatedly find the place in her heart that is capable of loving him and embracing him just the way he is.

Making It Easy to Communicate

Art said, "I could never figure out why Lindsay would talk so much about the same problems, particularly when there was nothing I could do about them. It was a relief to know that I am not expected to solve her problems. It made it so easy to communicate. If I could just listen and not have to solve her problems to make her feel better, then okay—I could do that.

> After a long day of solving problems, the last thing I want to do is come home to another list of problems I have to solve.

"After a long day of solving problems, the last thing I want to do is come home to another list of problems I have to solve. When she would talk about problems, I always thought I would have to do more before I could relax. Now I just listen and relax, knowing that for her to feel better she basically needs to feel heard."

Saying the Wrong Thing

Les learned to restrain his impulse to respond. "When Gloria talked about her day with the kids, whatever I said was the wrong thing. She would feel misunderstood, unappreciated, and attacked. I couldn't figure it out. She was the one who wanted to have more conversations, but every time we talked we would end up feeling frustrated. She complained that I didn't listen, but every time I said something it made it worse.

"I learned just not to say anything. After a while, when she would talk, I would just begin to space out. I would get really bored and tired. It all sounded the same and I just wasn't interested. When she read *Mars and Venus Together Forever,* everything started to change.

> She told me she really appreciated me listening to her talk about her feelings and that I really didn't have to say anything.

"She told me that she really appreciated being able to share her feelings and understood that it must be hard for me just to listen, particularly since she didn't want me to offer her solutions. She went on to let me know that if I just listened and didn't say anything it would still be helpful.

"Now I don't say anything. Knowing that I am helping her makes a big difference. I like it when she says, 'Thanks for listening—it really helps.' It's different now that I know I am giving her what she needs by just listening. I am slowly starting to connect more and be more aware of her life, and be interested. I've learned I don't have to solve her problems and she will feel better. Now we both look forward to being together. She feels I love her and I get to be helpful."

A Blueprint for Relationships

Danny understood why he and his wife argued. "We had been married for fourteen years. We loved each other but we would argue all the time. I thought Marsha was just being too negative. After a few years of counseling, we called it quits and separated. Then I read *Men Are from Mars*. For me, it was literally out of left field to hear that women needed to talk about their feelings and problems before they could get on to feeling happier and more loving.

It was literally out of left field to hear that women needed to talk about their feelings before they could get on to feeling happier and more loving.

"I had always viewed her 'feelings' as an unreasonable attempt to criticize me. Her feelings made me feel like she didn't appreciate anything I did. Learning about Venusians and their valid need to talk freed me to not take it so personally. I realized that I had been the negative one. She was just sharing her feelings and I was having a negative reaction. This then caused us to spiral downward, saying mean things about each other.

"I called her up and told her what I was learning. She was interested and we went out to dinner. It was great, suddenly we were agreeing. We had words to express our feelings and positive ways of supporting each other. Before, it was not that we didn't love each other, but that we couldn't communicate in a positive manner. I really wasn't listening.

"Now I use *Men Are from Mars* as a blueprint for our relationship. You can't build a house without a plan. I think I just gave up because I didn't know what to do. Now I have the plan to build our relationship. I want to thank you so much. You have given me back the most precious thing in my life."

Learning the Customs on Venus

Martha had comments to make on listening. "Recognizing that it was difficult for men to be great listeners helped me appreciate Roger's attempts at listening. Instead of feeling that he didn't care enough to listen, I now know that when he does give solutions, it is not that he doesn't care but that he has forgotten what I need.

> **When he gives solutions, it is not that he doesn't care but that he has forgotten what I need.**

"He is from Mars and is still learning the customs on Venus. Old habits take time to change. Instead of giving him a hard time, I just smile and say, 'I just need to be real Venusian right now, you don't have to say anything.' He doesn't get defensive but instead smiles and says, 'Oops.' And that's it. I go on and he listens."

He Apologized for Being So Insensitive

Margaret said, "When I would talk about things that bother me, Tom would say either 'What's the point?' or 'Don't start!' It would shut me down. After a while I just stopped liking him. After reading your book, he apologized for being so insensitive. He told me that he wanted to start listening and that he wouldn't cut me off. Wow! Everything changed. Now I really look forward to spending time with him. Not only do I love him, but I like him as well."

I Didn't Just Want Lip Service

Jessica had this story: "When I first heard John Gray talk about this, I didn't like it. The last thing I wanted was a man to listen to me if he didn't want to. I wanted a man to *want* to listen to me; I didn't just want lip service. I wanted a man who cared enough and really was interested in what I had to say. It seemed degrading to ask a man to listen when I could sense that he didn't want to. The thought of him occasionally nodding his head and mechanically saying, 'um-hum . . . um-hum . . . um-hum . . . really,' was not my idea of intimacy. But I tried it and I was amazed—I did feel better.

**I didn't want a man to listen
if he didn't really want to.**

"I liked being able to talk without being interrupted. It had never happened before. No finishing my sentences, no solutions, no defensive comments. It was great. Now instead of feeling that he doesn't want to listen, I know that he is willing to listen because he wants to help. He may not really *want* to listen, but he does *want* to help and for that I really feel loved!"

She Had the Problem, Not Me

Steve discussed his learning process. "Whenever I would get together with my ex-wife it was trouble. She said she couldn't talk with me. That was fine with me but we shared two wonderful children. It was tearing them apart to see their parents rejecting and resenting each other.

"I didn't have a problem communicating but

she did. After all, she was the one who wouldn't talk to me and I was a lawyer, a professional counselor. It was clear that I could put my feelings to the side and talk rationally. She had the problem, not me.

"I finally realized that if she didn't want to talk to me, then I must be a part of the problem. Using my legal interrogation skills, I was putting her on trial each time we talked. When she would share her feelings, I would interrupt repeatedly and correct her. I would explain away the reasons she felt upset about things. I would repeatedly invalidate her generalizations with counterexamples, without any consideration of her feelings.

**I was putting her on trial
each time we talked.**

"After reading your book, I wrote her a letter and apologized for being inconsiderate and told her that in the future I would try very hard to listen in a respectful way without making put-down comments. This one comment and realization transformed our whole relationship. I learned to leave my legal skills in the office and with her to just listen and try to understand the validity of her point of view—even if I disagreed. Now we are not only talking, but we are friends. Our children see their parents as loving and respectful of each other. What a special gift this message is."

I Don't Need to Be Fixed

Erica said, "Each time we argued about something, after a while we would end up arguing about the way we were arguing. He would say it was my problem that I was so unhappy and that if I would just live in the moment and appreciate what was good in my life, then I would feel much better. Then I wouldn't make such a big deal of things.

"I would say that he didn't understand, that he didn't care, and that it wasn't all my problem. I told him I couldn't talk with him if he kept trying to fix me. I needed him to share with me the responsibility for our problems and see the validity of my side.

> "It's okay if we disagree. I just need you to hear and understand my point of view."

"By understanding that men automatically want to solve problems, I was able to change my approach. Now, when we start to argue, it diffuses the tension when I first pause and then prepare him for what I want to say.

"I say, 'You don't have to agree with me. That's okay. I just need you to hear and understand my point of view. We don't have to solve this problem right away. If you just listen to me, then I can also hear what you have to say. That will make me feel much better.'

"When I do this he suddenly calms down and listens. We don't have to fight. He gets to be right and I get the right to share and express how I feel—without being interrupted, corrected, or fixed."

You Don't Understand

Paul shared, "My wife used to always complain, 'You don't understand!' She still does sometimes, but now it doesn't turn into an argument. Before we took your workshop, when she said I didn't understand I would argue and explain that I did. Sometimes I would even explain I understood what was bothering her better than she did. This definitely didn't work.

"One simple change made a world of difference. Now, when she says that I don't understand, I realize she is really saying that *she* needs to tell me more before I can fully understand. I have learned to say in response, 'Okay, you're right. I don't understand, tell me more.' This one change has stopped all our arguments.

"Okay, you're right. I don't understand, tell me more." This one change has stopped all our arguments.

"I have learned that when she has a chance to keep talking without my interrupting, inevitably she becomes more loving toward me. Although it takes a little more time than I would like, she does eventually feel more understood.

"It was hard for me to acknowledge that I didn't understand her, particularly when I thought I did. But I finally learned that when she doesn't feel understood, then I am definitely not understanding her in the way she needs. Simply to agree that I don't understand was really giving her the understanding she needed. To say she was right, and agree that I didn't understand, was in effect saying that I did understand that she doesn't feel understood. With this support she could then continue to share and explore what else she was feeling. My acknowledging that I didn't understand actually helped her to feel understood."

Giving Up Anger and Getting What I Needed

Jerry related his story. "The other day my wife was very concerned about some problems I was having at work. Normally I would have gotten very angry that she was giving me advice, doubting me, and really treading on my territory. Instead of getting angry, I practiced dodging and tried to not take her comments and fears personally.

> **Instead of getting angry, I practiced not taking her comments and fears personally.**

"I just let her talk and didn't get angry. I realized she was from Venus and her way of dealing with her fears was to talk about them. After giving her what she needed, I then asked her for what *I* needed: when she was done I said, 'I know you are afraid and it's important to talk about that. What I need to hear from you is that you trust me to take care of things and that you're glad that I'm here to handle things.'

"Having felt heard, she was able to then give me the support I needed. She very willingly said she trusted me and was so grateful we were together. I smiled and felt good as I hugged her, instead of feeling beaten down by her fears and feelings."

Alarm Signals

Sam shared his insights. "I have learned that when Tia acts in a cordial way but doesn't talk much, it is an alarm signal. It means something is brewing inside and if I don't get her to talk soon, it will just grow worse. When she seems distant, instead of just ignoring her I take notice. There is generally something that I've done or neglected to do, and it is building up inside her and preventing her from being loving.

When she seems distant, instead of just ignoring her I take notice.

"If I don't notice that she is upset, she feels that I don't care. And if she has to finally initiate a conversation to express her feelings, then she is much more upset and it takes a lot longer to get things resolved. My willingness to notice and ask her what's the matter goes a long way to resolve whatever feelings that are building up inside."

Going Fishing

Harvey tuned in to his wife's needs. "When Rebecca wants to talk the most, she acts like she doesn't even want to talk. Then, when I start a conversation, she'll start out saying there's not much to talk about.

"I say, 'Is something the matter?' and she says it's nothing. I used to just walk away thinking I had done my duty and now I could watch some TV. That was a big mistake.

"Now I've learned not to take her literally. When she says there's not much to talk about, I now hear that she wants to talk but needs me to ask her questions to gradually draw her out. Instead of walking away, I go fishing. I keep asking her questions until I get a bite.

....

Instead of walking away, I go fishing. I keep asking her questions until I get a bite.

....

"She doesn't just want me to listen, she wants me to notice that she probably needs to talk. She wants me to be tuned in to what's happening in her life, so that I already have a sense of why she is upset. She wants me to ask her questions that reveal that I know what is going on in her life.

Just as when you're fishing, it takes patience, but eventually I ask the right question and she begins to open up.

"I used to think that if she wanted to talk about something, then she should just come out and say it. That's how I am. But I am starting to understand that for Venusians it's a comforting feeling that someone cares and is watching out for them. I like being that guy."

I Listen Because I Love You

Wendy said, "The thing I love most about Gerald is his willingness to listen. When there is a problem we talk about it. Even though it would be much easier to gloss over it and watch TV, he is willing to sit down and listen. What I have to say sometimes is definitely not very nice, nor is it to the point. He doesn't always agree, nor is it very comfortable, but he does it anyway."

Gerald responded, "She sure is right about that. It's hard to hear her feelings; a part of me wants to run, but I stay because I have learned how important it is to her. Although I don't necessarily like what she is saying, I listen because I love her and I know she needs this support from me.

> It's hard to hear her feelings; a part of me
> wants to run, but I stay because I have
> learned how important it is to her.

"I even say to her, 'This is very difficult for me but I am willing to listen and consider your feelings because I love you.' Saying it out loud not only helps her feel my willingness to listen but makes it easier for me too. I suppose it helps me to remember once again that love is the answer and by listening I am giving her the love she needs. In the most effective way, I am doing what she needs most from me."

Anger Erupts When We Try to Talk

Bruce told his story. "We have been married for twenty years. It is a second marriage for both of us. We brought two families together—I brought three kids and she brought one. We raised all four children. We have had difficult communication problems since early in our marriage. There has been a great deal of mistrust and defensiveness. After the kids left, our marriage got worse and we semi-separated for a while. We have had separate bedrooms for years. A great deal of anger and resentment erupts when we try to talk, even about little things.

"When I read through your book, I saw things that sounded like what Gretchen had been saying to me for years. I had really never understood what she was talking about, or why it was such a big thing. I also saw stuff I had been trying to tell her, to no avail. I saw explanations for things I was experiencing but had not been able to visualize in a positive perspective. The hope for finally being able to communicate was exciting to me.

"Gretchen, however, was not so enthusiastic. Her response to me was: I will believe it when I see it. If you change, I will consider these ideas. Instead of getting defensive in response to her mistrust, I realized the validity of her feelings. After years of her feeling neglected, I am finding it takes time to heal and rebuild trust. I am also finding that my gentle persistence in caring enough to make changes and in learning how to listen is helping her to let go of her resistance, and is helping me too. It is not easy to start over and have your every step mistrusted and resisted. However, I am feeling stronger in the process, and I like that feeling.

> My gentle persistence was just what she needed to help her to let go of her resistance.

"When it doesn't seem to be working, instead of dumping my angry feelings on Gretchen, I start privately writing out and venting my feelings in a 'love letter,' as you suggest in your books. I start out feeling very angry and upset and end up feeling that I have achieved a release and begin to experience loving feelings again. These loving feelings help me to understand her perspective, and once again I try to be a better listener.

"My wife and I have had tender moments and brief periods of meaningful communication. However, we still sometimes keep our distance and keep our guard up. Even though we have a lot of negative history, there is hope. I have become much more excited about my life and for the possibilities within life.

"I can see more clearly now the problems in our relationship and I know what to do. I can see changes within me where I feel more loving of myself, of my wife, and of others. New people have been coming into my life and old friends have been returning. There is a new dimension to life that feels wonderful.

"Gretchen and I still upset each other. In such cases, I used to say, 'Oh, no, not this again! I wish she would somehow learn how to flow with life and get off my case!' Now I am getting to where I can say, 'Well, there is something more I need to learn. I am upset now and I know how to take care of it. I can go out and write a love letter or I can take some time to go for a walk and think things through a bit and calm down.'

"Although I don't enjoy getting upset and having to process these feelings, I always seem to get new insights about myself and my wife. As a result I am learning to be easier on myself and I hope on Gretchen as well. Through understanding in a positive way why we have been misunderstanding each other, I have found hope again. This has been an incredible journey."

Feeling Better About Myself

Renata shared, "Learning about our differences helped me feel better about myself as well. On the way home from a vacation in South Carolina, I began thinking out loud, stating what I had to do when I returned home the next week—and the next month, the next three months, and so on.

"I finished my sentence with, 'Yes, and in six months I have to go to the dentist.' Then what John Gray said regarding how women think came back to my mind—not only out loud but expanding outward too. He has made it all right for me to be the way I am.

"I have four sons, and they used to criticize

me for thinking out loud—they accused me of 'babbling.' But now I know I'm just being Venusian and thinking out loud."

Our Marriage Was Okay but Lacked Excitement

Ian described how he and his wife improved their communication. "Ten years ago Ellen wanted to take off on a romantic weekend. I was very much in love with my wife, but I'd been noticing a kind of sameness to our life—our sex, communication, dealings with our children. The marriage was okay, but there was a lack of excitement. It just seemed to me that the relationship wasn't being nurtured. There was love there—always—and commitment, no question. I knew I was going to remain married to Ellen for the rest of my life. Everything else was booming—business, and the kids—but in the marriage something had gone flat. My commitment was there, but from an emotional standpoint I felt that the tank was becoming empty.

"So I persuaded Ellen to give up on the vacation idea and go to a John Gray seminar. And in the first five minutes I knew we were in the right place. He started by talking about all the mistakes *he* had made in his relationships, and right away I felt a tremendous weight lift off my shoulders. I didn't have to be a perfect person! I didn't have to be responsible for making the relationship perfect, for creating our happiness. In the first two minutes, John's openness and self-disclosure made me feel right.

"And in the longer run, I gained an emotional language. My spiritual side was developed. My physical side was strong—I was a P.E. teacher. But I didn't really have an emotional language, and there were feelings I had that I was never able to describe or express.

"Certain kinds of communication had always been threatening to my sense of power as a man. I was vulnerable, afraid to express disappointments and unhappiness, because I thought that letting on that I felt such things would jeopardize the whole relationship. I thought I had to always have a solution for everything and be in complete control. I had to be a strong man for this marriage, didn't I?

> I thought I had to always have a solution for everything and be in complete control.

"But, to my amazement, with the communication tools John taught, everything just opened up and I felt a connection with my own self. I felt a tremendous burden disappear and insights began pouring into me from all levels. I felt freer than I had in a long, long time; I felt love for myself and for my wife beginning to flow again. And I felt a tremendous feeling of hope.

"What accounted for this great flow of feeling? I could finally give voice to feelings that I had never expressed before. I learned to first give Ellen a chance to talk. I stopped getting caught up in trying to change how she felt. I gave up trying to give solutions all the time. Instead I would listen and then, when she was done, I could share my thoughts, feelings, and experiences and she would listen.

"In a practical sense, the impact of that seminar—a permanent impact—was that when my wife and I argued we could come back to a balance point a lot more quickly than before. I wouldn't shut down for as long as I had—my pattern before had been to brood and be moody and go on and on with it. Now, the time I spent doing that dramatically decreased. With John's techniques, I could come back to a balanced, loving space without a fear of 'confrontation.'"

....

My pattern before had been to brood and be moody and go on and on with it.

....

"For example, if Ellen was doing something that bothered me, I would be able to tell her—rather than shoving those feelings down or (as in the past) raising my voice, trying to be more controlling with anger, and just blurting things out. This new avenue was more respectful, and involved listening both to Ellen's side and to *my* own voice inside.

"Once this became habit, it was obvious that these new communication skills actually worked. They provided me with a road map to guide myself on an emotional level. I could always do that on a physical, intellectual, and professional level, but now I had a path to the emotional level as well.

"*Everything* was affected. We became so much closer, the communication opened tenfold, and our sex life was enlivened to the point it had been in the beginning—and this continues today. But perhaps the most surprising impact of my new listening skills and understanding of gender differences came in my relationships with our son and daughter.

"Because I was more forgiving of myself and the mistakes I had made as a man and a parent, I became more patient with them, more compassionate, more supportive. Because I was now supporting myself and my spouse emotionally, I could do that with my children as well. Before that, I had taken a more dictatorial approach with them, though there was always love underneath. So, consequently, my children are very expressive with their own emotions and comfortable around peers and adults—more comfortable than I ever was. It's tremendously satisfying to see them getting the benefit of *my* own benefits from this work.

As a parent I became more patient, compassionate, and supportive.

"We have regular family meetings, and if a conflict arises, we now have ways of working things out. Based on John's techniques of listening, everybody gets heard. Anyone at any time can call a family meeting to express thoughts, and the children do that. They thrive on it, actually.

"So, you see, we have something to give them: our ways of communicating are our true gifts to our children. They see us communicating and growing, arguing but making up and apologizing, committed to each other to make it work, and hearing each other out. We know that every time we give to each other we are also giving to our children."

Love at First Sight

Ellen told her side. "It began twenty years ago. I was only twenty-four, and I had known this man for three weeks and decided I wanted to marry him. Three months later we were married.

"We were very similar, really. Ian's parents had divorced when he was fourteen, and my father had died when I was eleven. So we were both raised by single parents.

"For the first three years, we had lots of fun. We had our kids, and seven years later, by year ten, we weren't having sex a lot, and I was feeling a lot of anger. There just wasn't a lot of aliveness in our relationship, even though we were committed to it.

By year ten, we weren't having sex a lot, and I was feeling a lot of anger.

"Ian decided we needed to take a seminar from John Gray. Actually, I was afraid. I thought we might realize that we'd chosen the wrong mates, that I'd find I didn't love Ian or that he didn't love me.

"What happened was a total catharsis. We learned the tools that enabled us to be in this relationship. "The main tool for me as a woman was to become more vulnerable. I saw there that I was on the masculine side of life—always focused on solving everyone else's problems and ignoring my own needs and feelings. John showed us the way a woman needed to talk, talk, talk. And how that was the natural way for a woman.

"Second, and almost more personally profound for me, at that seminar I had a huge breakdown around my feelings of loss for my father. I had never experienced these feelings, but I began to cry about them, and John saw me crying and called me up to the front of the room. He asked me if I'd like to share my feelings, and this progressed into a catharsis about having felt abandoned by men, not being able to trust men, and feeling that I could not dare to be vulnerable to men. John called Ian up to hold me when I expressed my feelings about my father. Allowing Ian to be there to witness this was just an incredible experience for me!

"If we women could just *trust,* and teach men *not to try to fix but just to listen,* then our hearts would automatically open up and we would feel much closer to the men. This is what happened to me. That experience improved our whole relationship: our physical life, our intimacy, our relationship with the children. We stopped putting the children in the middle in order to keep our distance from each other.

> We have the tools to express our needs, feelings, likes, dislikes, and the format not to get hooked, not to take things so personally.

"Without John's seminar, I don't know where we would be. With it, though, we are life partners. We have the tools to express our needs, feelings, likes, dislikes, and the format not to get hooked, not to take things so personally. The format allows us, out of love, to be able to hear each other and try to support each other in what we are asking for and feeling.

"How do we make each other happy? Both of us try to keep the romance alive. We prioritize working on our relationship by taking time to have fun together. We take time away from the kids to be romantic and we take time away from each other to do things on our own. When we come back together, we are missing one another and have more to share.

"As for what I do for Ian to make him happy, well, he needs to be trusted—so I back off from giving him advice and suggestions unless he really asks. I try to appreciate him as much as I can for everything he does.

"What does Ian do to make me happy? He listens. He does caring little things for me. He brings me a cup of tea every morning. He participates greatly in the parenting. But the biggest thing is his incredible respect for me. He praises me and expects our children to act the same way. Those are the ways we make each other happy."

Talkers and Thinkers

This is Suzanne's story. "I am forty-seven years old and have been married for ten years. My husband, Rich, and I have known each other for twelve years and have no children.

"During the first several years of our marriage, I felt that there was not enough communication between us. I'm the 'talker' and Rich is the 'thinker' in the family.

"I would try and try to get him to open up and share his thoughts and feelings with me, but to no avail. I came from a previous marriage where there was no communication, and I was determined that this marriage was going to be different—or it would surely fail as well.

"Like many couples, we didn't know how to express ourselves. Rich didn't know how to verbalize what he felt, and I didn't know what words to use to get him to open up. I found myself getting more and more angry and frustrated; the laughter had gone out of our marriage.

As soon as I would begin to speak, I could see him shut down and become defensive.

"I would watch *Oprah* and get ideas on how to communicate better; then I would try to explain the techniques to Rich when he came home. As soon as I would begin to speak, I could see him shut down and become defensive. His defensiveness was extremely difficult for me to deal with. An argument would ensue. He would then make a small effort to be better for about a week or two and then we'd be right back where we started.

"My main concern, besides Rich's defensiveness, was that I was feeling taken advantage of and not being 'taken care of.' I wanted a man in my life who would take control once in a while. It seemed I was the one running the household, doing all the chores, doing all the worrying, and not even receiving so much as a thank-you for my efforts. My resentment was really beginning to build up. Rich always had clean underwear in his drawer and fresh shirts in his closet. Why couldn't

I open my drawer and closet to find my clothes ready to wear? I found myself falling out of love with my husband and didn't know where to turn.

"A disturbing habit was forming. Every few weeks, when it all became too much, I would attempt to explain to him what I was feeling, but all I would do was cry. He would promise to do more around the house; again, it only lasted a week or so.

"Then I heard about your book, *Men Are from Mars, Women Are from Venus*. I was reading the book when I heard you were speaking in New York City. I asked Rich if he would go, and he did. It was the best thing that could have happened for us!

"As you spoke, he heard *my* words coming out of *your* mouth. He saw us in everything you were saying. The most important thing you spoke about was what really turns women on—taking out the trash, washing the dishes, folding the laundry, etc. Rich was amazed at that; I suppose a lot of men are. We talked about it on the way home, and since that night our relationship has not been the same.

As you spoke, he heard *my* words coming out of *your* mouth. He saw us in everything you were saying.

"Now, without being asked, Rich takes out the trash, takes the recycling to the curb, washes dishes, folds laundry, vacuums, handles all the bills, etc., etc. And I thank him when he does these things for me.

"We keep communications open, but it takes work. It doesn't always happen spontaneously. He takes the time to listen to me, even when it is not what he wants to be doing. If I read Rich's face and can tell there is something on his mind, or I may have said something he didn't like, I encourage him to tell me what he's thinking. If he doesn't want to talk, then I don't press. I think, however, that because he doesn't feel pressured he is much more willing to share what's going on.

> I encourage him to tell me what he's
> thinking. If he doesn't want to talk,
> then I don't press.

"We tell each other 'I love you' every day. We don't leave the house or arrive home without kissing each other hello or good-bye. One thing Rich has always done since I met him is to call me at least once a day, just to see how I'm doing, and he always tells me when I can expect him home.

"This brings to mind something that happened the other day. I was baking cookies for Christmas and accidentally put in twice the amount of baking soda the recipe called for. I began baking, and the first batch of cookies tasted salty. I had to throw out the entire batch of dough and start all over again. Naturally, I didn't have enough ingredients to make another batch, so I had to run to the store.

"Before leaving, I asked Rich if he would help me when I returned, and he said, 'Why don't you do it tomorrow?' That's not the answer I was looking for. I said nothing, and went to the store. When I returned ten minutes later, he must have given some thought to what he said to me, because he met me at the door and said, 'I'll help you. Just tell me what you want me to do.'

"A feeling of total happiness came over me. Two years ago, he would have sat in his recliner while I baked the second batch.

Two years ago, he would have sat in his recliner while I baked the second batch.

"As I said before, it takes constant work. Bad habits die hard. What makes me so happy is that now both of us really work at making the other happy. If we unintentionally say or do something that may make the other sad or angry, we acknowledge that we were wrong, apologize, and make it right.

"We're the happiest we've ever been, and it keeps getting better."

5

The Martians
Are Coming

As I travel around the country teaching seminars, I am deeply touched to hear stories of couples separated or even divorced who, after reading my books, have reunited in a loving relationship. Although it was not uncommon to hear these kind of stories from participants in my relationship seminars, I never imagined merely reading one of my books and applying its ideas could have such an impact.

With so many divorces today, it is an inspiration to hear stories of Martians and Venusians coming back to love. In healing a wounded relationship or solidifying a commitment to marriage, there are generally many factors at work, which can be very confusing. It begins to make sense, however, when we understand the differences between men and women.

How Men Grow in Love

Men grow in love as a result of getting close and then pulling away. Like a rubber band, a man stretches back before eventually springing back. The old saying "Distance makes the heart grow fonder" aptly describes a man's ability to love. In a back-and-forth motion, he gradually grows in love. Repeatedly, women have discovered that by letting go, their men have come back more loving than before.

> **"Distance makes the heart grow fonder"**
> aptly describes a man's ability to love.

When a relationship ends, or is about to end forever, a man sometimes gets the distance he needs to discover how much he loves his partner; he is then motivated to begin again. All he needs is an understanding of what went wrong and how it can be fixed. Without this insight, however, he may not allow himself to go back.

Many men regret the end of a relationship but resign themselves to it because they don't know what went wrong. A man gives up in a relationship when he feels he can't make the woman happy. The basic insights of *Men Are from Mars,* however, are enough for him to realize what went wrong and how to fix it. This insight allows him to recommit himself to making it work.

How Women Grow in Love

Women grow in love when they feel they can get the support they need. They give up in a relationship when communication breaks down. Like a wave, a woman crashes but is unable to rise again in love. Without nurturing communication, a woman begins to feel unloved. Over time she feels that she is doing all the giving and not getting what she needs. As a result, she begins to resent her partner. She feels that she has nothing left to give, and because she also feels powerless to get what she needs, she leaves.

The more she resents her partner, the more she feels trapped into feeling that her happiness is dependent on him. Through separation she is free to feel responsible for getting her needs fulfilled. If she has the opportunity to experience getting what she needs from her friends and family, the wave rises and she discovers again her loving feelings.

In a healthy way, she is able to get her needs met from her friends, discovering that she can be happy without her partner. Feeling more autonomous and self-assured frees a woman to forgive and forget. Then, with a new understanding of how she can get what she needs in a relationship, her heart can open once again to loving and trusting.

In thousands of cases, the basic insights of *Men Are from Mars* have helped women to see their part in the problems that afflict the failing relationship. They realize that they were loved more than they believed. With this deeper understanding of men, women do not feel so powerless to successfully get the love and support they need to continue giving and loving. Along with a healthy sense of responsibility, this newfound confidence has saved marriages.

> **Feeling more autonomous frees a woman to forgive and forget.**

For many women, the ideas from *Men Are from Mars* have been enough to inspire them to find love again. Quite often a woman discovers that her love for her partner is rekindled and comes back stronger than before. She realizes that it was not that he didn't love her, but that he was from Mars and didn't know how to give her the support she needed. She was from Venus and didn't understand the way men think and feel differently.

The Challenge of Love

Following upon a man's renewed willingness to provide the support a woman needs or a woman's realization that she can get the support she needs, thousands of couples have reunited in love. Their stories are truly an inspiration, because they speak to the highest part of ourselves: that part within us that intuitively knows our true purpose on our journey in this world is to find love and be loving. This is our challenge; to achieve it brings out all that is inherently good and great about being human. The triumphs of these couples mirror our own each time we recommit ourselves to love. Although some of these stories describe couples getting back together after a separation or divorce, the same principles apply each time we take a step closer in love.

He Hated It and Just Left One Day

With tears in her eyes, Annette told her story. "We were divorced and then my husband, Bruce, read your book. I can't express to you how happy we are now. We now have a baby girl and are so happy. For years we argued. He worked for the airlines and when he came home he would be distant. I would always try to bring us back together through talking. He hated it and finally just left one day.

"Six months after we were divorced, he read your book. He called me and told me about the cave idea and then said he realized why talking was so important to me. He had missed me so much, but just didn't know what to do. Your book gave him the courage to try it again. We listen to your tapes and read your books again and again. We are so grateful to be happily married."

I Loved Her but I Wasn't in Love

Tom shared, "We had been married twenty-three years. I loved Christy but I wasn't in love with her. We would never want to hurt each other but we weren't happy together. Everything was flat. There was nothing to talk about anymore. I wanted our divorce to be amicable. Although we had been to various counselors, she asked that we attend a John Gray seminar, just to see if there was anything we could do to save our marriage.

"I was sure that it was over but to make her feel better I said yes. Within the first hour my mind was changed. I couldn't believe my ears. You were describing our relationship over the past twenty-three years. Except that now it was making sense. For so long I had tried to be the loving partner but I didn't give myself what I needed.

"I had secretly felt there was nothing I could do to ever make Christy happy. I, like most men, thought I was supposed to solve her problems and didn't realize that she just needed to feel heard and be reassured that I cared. I had turned off years ago, because nothing I said ever made a difference.

I had turned off years ago, because nothing I said ever made a difference.

"Over the years she began to wilt. She always said that she loved me, but it seemed that whatever I did was never enough. Now I understood why: I wasn't listening. She always complained that we didn't talk, but there was nothing to talk about. That's all changed now. We can talk about everything because we are not afraid of hurting each other. We can talk about our feelings with a much greater understanding. I have learned to listen more and she is much happier. We are in love again and look forward to staying in love for the rest of our lives."

Rebuilding Trust

Jacob said, "After reading *Men Are from Mars,* I thought I could go back to my wife and make things better. We had mutually decided to end our marriage. I was convinced that through applying these new ideas we could make it work. Theresa was not convinced.

"After many discussions we moved back in together, but still she was not sure. I had made many mistakes for a lot of years and she wasn't convinced that I could change. It took about six months but gradually she warmed up and started to trust me. Although I didn't like having to wait that long, rebuilding the trust helped me solidify what I needed to learn about relationships.

Rebuilding the trust helped me solidify what I needed to learn about relationships.

"My problem was that I wanted things on my terms. I thought her terms were unreasonable. When she was upset about something or just less than friendly and positive, I would go to my cave and pout. I would withhold my love for days; then, once I was out of my cave, I would behave as if nothing had happened. Repeatedly she was left feeling incomplete. We would argue, I would walk out, and then nothing would be said again.

"Her unwillingness to trust me forced me to prove to her that I could do it differently. I realized that when things didn't go my way I would just shut down and behave in an uncaring way. I still shut down and withdraw to my cave, but the one difference now is that when I come out I am very attentive, affectionate, and I will open up the conversation again and take the time to understand and validate her point of view.

"With this new insight into why she mistrusted me, I was able to show her through my actions that I cared. She was able to gradually open up and love me again. We are so happy today and it feels great knowing I have the power to keep it that way."

Let's Just Be Friends

Will explained, "My girlfriend, Sara, decided that she wanted to just be friends and that she wanted to date other men. I didn't know what to do. Was I just to smile, put my tail between my legs, and walk away or what? Was I supposed to get angry and fight for her love? I was so confused. I thought I had been doing everything the right way.

"After reading *Mars and Venus Together Forever*, I realized that I had been *too* intimate. The focus in the relationship had always been me. I would go to her and tell her what was going on in my life. I was always calling her. I thought this is what women wanted and also what I wanted.

I think I learned the hard way that "Mr. Sensitive" can be a real turnoff.

I think I learned the hard way that "Mr. Sensitive" can be a real turnoff. Instead of going to her and sharing my hurt and abandoned feelings, I decided to try writing my feelings. As you suggested, every time I would start to miss her I would write out a letter expressing my feelings of anger, sadness and hurt, fear, and guilt. After writing my negative feelings I would then focus on expressing understanding, forgiveness, and love. Not only did this help me find relief, but eventually I started to realize how self-centered and demanding I was. There was no room in our relationship for her feelings.

"After waiting a few weeks, I gave her a casual call to see how she was doing. She was very hesitant to talk. I set her at ease by making sure she didn't have to feel guilty for dumping me. Instead of focusing on telling her how I was feeling, I stayed upbeat and kept leading the conversation to her. I asked her questions and instead of reacting I just listened. After a few more weeks and a few more calls, I invited her to lunch. She agreed and now, about a year later, we are engaged to get married. It's hard to believe that one small change could make such a big difference."

Making a Commitment

Keith shared, "Janet and I dated for a year or so, and then we reached a critical point: Would we commit to the relationship or not? Would we get married?"

Janet: I didn't want to get married, as a matter of fact. But I definitely wanted a commitment from

Keith. But Keith didn't want to promise to give up seeing other women, not then.

Keith: It was interesting. We couldn't resolve the issue. At that time, I'd known John Gray for longer than I'd known Janet, and we had a phone consultation with him. He upheld and reflected back our positions without favoring either one, and it was amazing.

"Keith," he said, "you want to have other experiences, date other women, kind of play the field." "Right," I agreed. "And, Janet, you want monogamy from Keith. Your needs for a clear commitment from Keith aren't being met." It was very interesting to hear him empowering Janet in this way by saying, you know, you're entitled to this, you're entitled to want a clear-cut commitment from me.

Janet: Right. John said to me, "Did you hear what Keith said? He just said he isn't ready to commit to a monogamous relationship with you. Is that all right with you? Can you live with that and still have the relationship?" I had to say no, I couldn't.

Keith: So John said, "You've got a statement here. It sounds to me as if you have to separate. You have to choose."

I guess this was what we knew, but John just described the situation more forcefully, more clearly than we had seen it, so that especially Janet could hear what she didn't want consciously to acknowledge.

Janet: Yes, he made the situation clearer and stated it so that we could own the truth of the relationship. It was a hard lesson, a lesson about honesty, which we all know is a big part of things. But once you decide you want to be honest, how you actually go about being honest isn't that simple.

Keith: Right. But John was correct; we couldn't reconcile our positions. So we did part ways.

Janet: I was sad about not being together anymore. Still, though, going through with the separation was empowering to me, because it said, okay, you're not getting your own needs met the way things are going, so you have to make a change. I think in many relationships people just go along with the flow. But John presented me with the idea that I had my needs and was entitled to them. So it was very difficult to face the idea of not being together, since we really did love each other, but we just weren't ready to go to the next level.

> We really did love each other, but we just
> weren't ready to go to the next level.

Keith: Clearly, empowering Janet was basic, but John also helped me by not making me wrong for wanting to play the field. It's subtle, you know. The conclusion was that I wasn't a bad person for having those feelings. So Janet and I went our separate ways, and though things didn't work out so great for me "in the field," still, I got to explore what I wanted without being judged harshly for wanting it.

Janet: That separation was very hard. We saw each other a couple of times during that six months and I just cried. I remember one night when there was . . . how should I put it . . . the opportunity for intimacy. It was very upsetting, but I really knew I had to hold out. I told myself, I'm worthy of commitment, I'm entitled to it, so if I can't have it, well . . .

Keith: Oh, yes, I remember that night, and other situations too. I had a lot of respect for Janet for standing behind her convictions. It gave me even more respect for her than I had before—and it made her even more desirable.

Janet: So six months later, we did get back together, and there was lots of excitement around that. And when it finally happened, our relationship was wonderful. We could finally relax. We did start to have a committed relationship.

When we finally got back together, our relationship was wonderful.

Keith: And honesty never became a problem. Before it hadn't really been an issue either—it was two honest people trying to figure out what to do. And honesty is no guarantee that you won't have problems. Still, I think ever since we finally came together, we've had an extremely high level of honesty.

Janet: One of the things that helped us during those early times was the love-letter technique. We did so many—and that helped us to be as open as we could be. When we got back together, we wrote and wrote those letters and then shared them with each other. Writing and reading the letters gave us a platform for being honest. It's one thing to commit to being honest and another actually *to be* honest. Everybody knows how difficult it is to say, "You know, I can't stand when you . . ." It's lots easier to communicate that sort of thing in a loving way in a letter.

Keith: Still, for us the love letters were never really an easy option. We would have a fight and go round and round, and even in the letter it would be uncomfortable to tell how we felt. The comfort came from getting to the other side. Most of the time, at the end of the letter we didn't have everything solved. But mostly the letter created a release. In John's seminars, I've seen all kinds of couples do love letters who would just embrace the idea, dashing the letters off in their spare time. But that wasn't us: even reading them to each other was uncomfortable. But we would get through it.

The letters work. They're powerful, and all this stuff surfaces in a safe format. Meanwhile, you're learning: if I have something going on with my wife and it looks kind of ugly, it doesn't have to be edited out of existence. In fact, it can't be. So the letters educate you about how to work with emotions.

If I have something going on with my wife and it looks kind of ugly, it doesn't have to be edited out of existence.

When my parents fought, they wouldn't talk for weeks; and when it all blew over, you wouldn't talk about that bad stretch at all. But with the letters you can actually work with these difficult emotions in an active, positive way, and learn how to get better at doing that.

Janet: Eventually we got engaged, we got married, and we had a baby. I'd say that before we had the baby, we really worked on communication, though I was resistant. Whenever an issue came up and we needed to deal with it, I'd be looking for a way to get out, thinking, I'm not dealing with this, I'm out of here.

Keith: But we had John Gray's tools, which are subtle but powerful. So a fight would come up and we could say, eventually, "We know how to get out of this." Maybe we couldn't work it out right on the spot, but we'd know that we could do it.

Janet: The best thing for me was learning to talk about how I feel. Keith can hear me a lot better when I'm just talking about feelings and not pointing my finger at him.

Keith: It's true. She knows how to say what she wants and isn't shy about asking for that, and usually she does it in such a way that conveys a lot of respect for me. So in this communication format we've developed for working out conflicts, we both get what we want.

Janet: When the baby came, I found it was hard to communicate openly and honestly when she was right there. I just didn't want to have a hard tone around her. I wanted to be respectful of her. Once or twice I've been explosive or reactive with Jennifer around, and she started to cry.

> **When the baby came, it was hard to communicate openly and honestly when she was right there.**

Keith: You know, most of the time we've had a wonderful time with our baby. But when she cries in reaction to us, well, she's like this little innocent thermometer, telling us what we're doing to her environment. So now there's an even higher premium on having good communication skills. I feel strongly that these very early years leave the deepest imprints on relationships. It's so important that we honestly create the kind of relationship environment for Jennifer that we want her to have.

> When she cries in reaction to us, well, she's like this little innocent thermometer, telling us what we're doing to her environment.

Janet: But it's not just Jennifer who's affected. There's been lots to deal with together since we had her. Her needs do fall more in my lap: I'm nursing, I'm home, and I have to keep remembering to ask for Keith's help. He just doesn't see the stuff I see, and it's a pain for me to ask him to, for instance, fill the vaporizer or something small like that. But either I ask him to do it, and feel supported that he does do it, or I carry it around as a little thing to be resentful about.

Keith: "Small things." It's a loaded term, because in the male world maybe these things are small. John talks about doing small things for each other—flowers, cards, and so forth—and I've found that they enrich not just Janet's life but our life together. It's funny, we finally managed to get a baby-sitter and get away, and suddenly in the parking lot I remembered that I used to open the car door for Janet. So I opened the door, and felt like, Oh, yes, I used to do this—this is great.

Janet: I definitely noticed. It was kind of silly and ridiculous, but it was fun, and sort of historical, taking us back to our courting days. Keith was showing that he wanted to take care of me, put a little icing on the cake. And I certainly do like icing.

Keith: See, the things are so little that they could seem trivial, but I think that they are what relationships survive on.

Janet: In a way, something like opening the car door for me is like glorious foreplay. It's romance. We are so busy with work and the baby, but we're trying to take care of ourselves. We're clear that it's important to make time for sex and romance. We need to be happy and healthy in our relationship in order to be good parents.

We need to be happy and healthy in our relationship in order to be good parents.

Keith: Totally true. In turbulence sometimes, it ain't just about communication. It's real clear to me that what's really happening is that we've gone too long without having connected on an intimate level.

Here's another thing about sex: for me as a male, the importance of taking time and being patient in sex has been an ongoing lesson. Taking time is equivalent to creating intimacy and a quality experience.

Janet: For me the big improvement in our sex life has been being more honest. Keith's thing is time—going slower—and for me it's honesty: telling him what feels right, and what doesn't feel right, tactfully and gracefully. It's easy to be shut down communication-wise in sex, but if we're really conscious and aware of each other's vulnerability, then we can really open up. The sex is the glue that holds us together.

Keith: You know, I have this friend who calls me almost weekly for advice on his relationships. It makes it so clear to me what it is I know. Lots of making the relationship work is just common sense. What's real to me is working things out with my wife and coming to understand her more. Love actually becomes this very humble, mundane thing, a process of working things out on a practical level. We have an argument, an old pattern arises, and there we are trying, continually working on getting things back to a harmonious state. I start to feel that yes, we will make it for the long term. No doubt about it.

Janet: True. I can't imagine us not being married. Even though we have our share of fights and spats, we do have a strong foundation and a commitment to the marriage. We'll go through what we need to go through to make it work. And I guess the big thing is, we have the tools. Those tools don't stay out in the garden shed. We use them.

Setting Standards

Cherie wanted to do it right. "We met *again* at our twenty-year high school reunion. Ken had graduated in '73 and enlisted in the Navy right out of high school. I had gotten pregnant and dropped out of school my freshman year. I would return to school ten years later and graduate from college with a degree in dental hygiene.

"By the time we met at that reunion, we had both been married twice. Ken had one child, a teenager, and I had two children: one grown and one seven. I had been single for almost eight years without any serious relationships, only a date or two here and there. Both of my marriages lasted less than a year. In the first one, when I was fourteen, needless to say, we were too young. And the second, when I was twenty-nine, was an abusive relationship from the beginning.

"Ken's first marriage ended because of his wife's infidelity; the other ended when they decided after a few months that they were better off as friends.

"At the reunion, I recognized Ken right away, even though you would never say we were friends, merely acquaintances in school. He was more the boy-next-door type in high school, nothing to get me excited at age fourteen. But when he looked down at me at the reunion and spoke with such a calm, assuring voice, I was delighted. He sat down and for at least an hour and a half we talked of our childhood, children, marriages, and the last twenty years of our lives. I remember thinking, This is really a nice guy.

"Next day, I figured I had nothing to lose, so I called him. Well, he came over that night. We talked for hours, watched movies with my seven-year-old son, who said at one point when Ken leaned over to kiss me, 'That's enough of that, Missy!' We were so stunned we all started laughing. Ken ended up spending the night. I told him later it all hinged on one word. When I asked him jokingly, 'Will you still respect me in the morning?' he said, *'Absolutely!'* Now that's my favorite word!

"The next day he left, as previously planned, to go back to school in Oregon to become a building inspector. I pursued him relentlessly with cards and phone calls. I went up to see him a month later and he came back with me for a couple of weeks. We went on a cruise, and my son, who was with us, was somewhat jealous but really liked Ken too. After the cruise, Ken went back to Oregon, but came back again for Thanksgiving and never left.

"We lived together for over a year. We were very compatible, sexually and otherwise, and he was good with my son and for my son. Over the first six months, although we got along, I felt somewhat used, because Ken didn't contribute much to the finances. I had many bouts with depression, and finally after six months I laid the cards on the table. I said I felt used because he didn't offer to pay much toward our cohabitation. It's true that he was also going through a crisis because he had just retired from the Navy after twenty years and now felt somewhat lost. He was not working but had his Navy retirement pay. I, on the other hand, had a very good-paying job, so it wasn't so much the money as the principle. After that, he did contribute, and things were somewhat better—but there was something else.

"Ken told me from the beginning that he would not tell me he loved me until he was sure. He *said* he was committed to our relationship but still could not say he loved me. And so my depression continued. It's very hard on one's self-esteem when your friends ask you 'How are things going?' and all you can say is, 'I don't know.'

> He *said* he was committed to our
> relationship but still could not say
> he loved me.

"Finally, in September, I said, 'If you don't know if you love me by now, you'd better move out until you can figure it out.' Ken seemed to think that love was a 'feeling' that he wasn't sure he had for me.

"Ken moved out and was away on a job for almost a month. When he came back I told him we could not pick up where we left off, because my self-esteem could not handle it and it was too hard on my son, who was really attached to Ken by then.

"We saw a little of each other, but it was strained.

"Then we were watching TV one night and one of John Gray's infomercials came on. Dr. Gray was funny and entertaining and said everything I was feeling. I said to Ken, 'That's what we need,' meaning the tapes. Ken picked up the phone and ordered them right then and there. I couldn't believe it! To me, it was such a positive, unselfish move, and I was thrilled.

"We were very serious about the tapes and started listening to them every night. We'd stop in the middle of a tape and talk about it or rewind and listen again. Finally Ken understood how I felt. He was, and is, so good about listening and wanting to change what needs to be changed (now he brings me flowers all the time, something he never did before). I, on the other hand, realized how Martians think. Before that, I'd say to myself, 'How stupid can he be, not understand how hurt I've been?'

"We are now happily married and all I know is that our relationship would not be where it is today if not for the tapes—we both feel that way. Although we are not perfect, what we have is strong and focused. I think that, because we both have had bad experiences in the past, we appreciate more about what we have now than we could in previous relationships. We have our problems and fights, but we have a good life, and I'm so grateful for this man."

A Manual for Relationships

Sandy told a cross-generational story: "It's been two years now since I read your book *Men Are from Mars, Women Are from Venus*—the best book I've ever read to help me understand Wes and myself. It was as if you had written it for us alone. Someone had left the book at the Al-Anon office in Tyler, Texas, where I was working that day, and I gobbled up fifty pages that morning! The phone never rang, so I was able to really enjoy the book without interruption.

"I called my daughter and read her the part about Tom and Mary getting lost on a trip and Mary telling him to ask for directions. My daughter said, 'Gee, Mom, so that's what I've been doing wrong!' Ha! Then I called my husband, Wes, and he said, 'Would you take that manual with you on our next trip?'

"I don't argue with him about it, but he knows I think it's silly not to ask directions. We joke about it now and he will ask directions a little sooner.

"I bought five copies of the book and gave one to each of our three grown children with this inscription inside:

Your dad and I haven't been very good role models to you, especially when you were growing up, because we didn't have "God's Best" in our marriage relationship, but we hope this book will help you to be more successful in your "happily ever after-ing."

"At the time, our son's fiancée started reading the book and couldn't put it down—took it home with her. John laughed and told me she was telling him something later and said, 'Now, I'm not trying to tell you what to do or anything. . . .' Ha! They are happily married now and are a very compatible couple. I'm pleased that a book like yours could give them a little insight into what it takes to have a good relationship.

"My husband is a recovering alcoholic with five years' sobriety, and I've wasted many years trying to get him to 'come out of his cave.' Even in sobriety, he has barely ventured out. I feel more motivated about letting him be in his cave now, and this is wonderful. It never dawned on me to just let him do that and not worry about it. Your book redirected me about changing what I can—and that's only *me*.

"Still, it's been hard for me to let go of my expectations. I always thought that in sobriety, we would sit down and talk. Wrong!

"When I was little, I was in a foster home for ten years. Later, when my family was reunited, my parents never bothered to consider my feelings about that time apart. To me, this was abandonment, pure and simple, and having Wes withdraw to his cave seemed the very same. See, it seemed like déjà vu all over again, but when I read your book I understood a little more about how men, all men, need to withdraw to sort things out.

"I've gradually been working on letting go of

my expectations. My prayer has been that I'd be quieter and love my husband unconditionally. A problem has been that my voice tends to rise when I'm angry—and that backs him into his cave—and *that* brings on my feelings of abandonment; so that scenario has repeated itself over and over in our marriage.

"Recently, something different happened. We're temporarily living in a trailer in California on his job assignment, and I decided we needed to talk again. I had to keep my voice down, because the neighbors were so close. He didn't leave, because unlike at home, he didn't have a lake to fish in. So we were both forced into different behavior. He related to my feelings more than usual and I was more accepting of him. Also, I remembered to keep the conversation short, and that helped.

"It was a real productive conversation, which didn't end with a 'ticking time bomb' or a 'closed clam'! It ended with a hug and love for each other. Since then, I've felt a great deal more peaceful and contented, and more love for the one I've chosen to have a lifetime relationship with. Anger, bitterness, and resentment dropped back a few more notches behind me and I felt myself move ahead a little more—and letting go.

"Your book is the most practical one I've ever found for understanding the differences between males and females—and it's so funny! I loved the comparison conversations too—right way, wrong way.

"My husband hasn't read the book, and that's okay. I'll still be eternally grateful to you for what I've gotten out of it. And thanks for the open sharing of what you and Bonnie went through in your relationship. It helps to know you're not just writing *about* something, but that you actually worked this out in your own life.

"I've told my Al-Anon friends and others to get your book. It's a winner. Thanks again."

Recognition!

Jeanette: "When I bought *Men Are from Mars, Women Are from Venus,* I cried and cried when I read chapter 7, 'Women Are Like Waves.' My husband had never been around a woman who is like a wave before me and used to tell me I was crazy. Learning that I was normal, and having him read the book, was a *great* experience.

My husband used to tell me I was crazy.
Learning that I was normal, and having him
read the book, was a *great* experience.

We respect each other so much more today than ever before. We thank God, therapy, and your book for helping us to figure it all out."

Running on Three Cylinders

Marie described being numb in marriage and overcoming a family crisis. "When I first got John Gray's book, I started learning so much about myself and our relationship. I felt like a baby getting wonderful milk from that book. I took it everywhere with me.

"John directly talked about what was worrying me so much. The foundation of our marriage had been all snowed over, to where my husband, Doug, and I were numb to one another.

"Now, I'm an interesting person. I've always got some exciting, adventurous thing going on. Even if I'm making mashed potatoes, I can make them sound so exciting that my husband can't wait to come home. My husband has always been very drawn to that, because he's a businessman. I'm a draw to him because I love life so much.

"But something was gone from us—we'd lost something we'd had at the beginning. We loved each other, always, but we weren't working on eight cylinders. We were working on about three cylinders. We loved each other, cared about each other, but we didn't have any feelings.

"Now, what was going on?

"Well, we had had a crisis. We were very high in love. Whenever we compared ourselves to our friends, it was clear to them and to us that we loved each other very much. But the company my husband was with, making a very comfortable six-figure income, folded its doors suddenly, and we had to change our lifestyle. Doug went into his cave, and because I wanted the nurturing and the comforting and the 'Don't worry, honey, everything's going to be all right,' I followed him right in there. I thought I was helping him, going after him like that. I thought I was the greatest wife in the world. I've read the stories of powerful women . . . why, Edison's wife got all the funding for his work. I just thought I was helping Doug, going in after him like that.

When I went in his cave, I thought I was the greatest wife in the world.

"It was then that I discovered John Gray's book. A friend talked to me about *Men Are from Mars, Women Are from Venus,* and I remembered, because if there was ever any marriage I respected, it was hers: a loving, caring example. When I saw the book in a store, I asked a friend to split it with me . . . until I saw what I was doing and had a talk with myself. 'Marie, you love your husband so much and you're going to split the cost of the book? Get serious!' And, financial crisis or no financial crisis, I bought the book. Reading it, I saw that I had been damaging Doug, really damaging him, so much. I was assuming that because he was in the cave he had pulled away and left me, left the whole family. And all along he was trying to sort things out and protect us as best he could. I didn't have a clue to that before.

"I just thought Doug was broken. And I'd thought this a lot of times before. I myself am a creative communicator and have developed some of my own tricks to get other people to share how they feel. But my own husband never shared his feelings, not with me or anybody. When he retreated—into his cave, as I know now—I called that 'being divorced.' I thought it was a serious infraction, and I would accuse him: 'I don't understand why you've divorced me. We love each other and you leave me. I can't get three words out of you.' We were very high in love, but on the inside I was never really sure that he liked me. And I know now that he wasn't quite sure I approved of him. He thought he probably wasn't a very good husband.

When he retreated—into his cave, as I know now—I called that "being divorced."

"All misinformation. Complete misinformation.

"The next thing that I found out I didn't know had to do with myself. Now, I'm a very smart and successful businessperson—very strong in that area. And I believed—the biggest mistake of all!—that it was my business sense that my husband loved and respected in me. But that love and respect didn't have a thing to do with the business side of me. In fact, now I see that side was a detriment to our marriage. I sure didn't know that, though. I was afraid to give it up, afraid to change, worried that I'd lose something.

"After the book I went to one of John's seminars, and he did something very small there, so small I think the other women might have missed the meaning of it. He had the women do a 'tweet, tweet, tweet'—that was our sound—and the men do a growl. To me, suddenly, those tweets coming out of me, those sweet sounds, were just so important. I had thought that by making them I'd lose something in my marriage, but no: I tweet now. I was a very macho gal, but now I tweet—just like I tweeted when Doug and I were dating. After that seminar I took a chance to act again like a lovely childlike girl, and suddenly I had a husband who oohed and aahed over me and who put his arm around me at the movies.

I had a husband who oohed and aahed over me and who put his arm around me at the movies.

"So where are we now? Big surprise, in the middle of another big change: our son Richard has AIDS. But between Doug and me there's a new understanding. I don't feel as if he's divorcing me when he goes into his cave. In fact, when he does that it makes me proud because I know that he's a man, and I feel secure when he's in there. I don't want to go into that cave. I don't want to hurt the inside of him. And I feel that I'm so lucky, because I don't think many women would have gotten away with what I got away with and still have their men fall back in love with them.

"We're strong enough now to turn to this

new situation with our son, who has come back home. He and I talk and talk. It has been absolutely the most rewarding experience of my life this year to be with my son. He is a gentle spirit and a beautiful person, and he is searching for the beauty of who he is. What I have learned from John Gray about Doug and about men and women now helps me to understand what a wonderful person I gave birth to.

"In searching and studying his own life, Richard has told me that he has felt inadequate about many things. But from what I've learned I have understood that he is one of the strongest people, the strongest men, I have ever known. John's work has helped me to show Richard his strengths—to touch unconditionally, to feel and be sensitive, to go to scary places where his brother wouldn't go, to say no when he means no, yes when he means yes, to see and appreciate the joy in my eyes that I've had from learning the truth. Richard loves John Gray because he sees that joy—and it's a gift to have joy when a child is sick, and to face a child's death without bitterness.

John's work has helped me to show my son his strengths.

"So John Gray has given me all of the beginning things I had with Doug when we first fell in love. And he's given me the softness that I had then too. He's given me the eyes and understanding to be with Richard, to talk with him every single day, just as if he were three years old and he had climbed up onto my lap. All that's wrapped up together.

"Doug's still quiet, quieter than ever. He still doesn't express himself much. But just this morning, which is almost Christmas, he came in and said, 'Here's the best present I'm giving you, Marie. I'm giving you this morning and all the other mornings for you to talk with Richard.' Absolutely right. He's made my life safe so I can talk as much as I need and want to with Richard.

"All my life, and I'm fifty-six, I've looked for how to be a woman, wife, and mother. John Gray has taken the pieces of the puzzle and pulled them all together.

"Anyway it seems like everything worked out.

"The funniest thing happened! We bought a car from some friends of ours and drove back from Georgia separately. I had a John Gray tape that I put in the new car, and Doug took the car and drove off . . . and found out—ha!—he couldn't turn off the tape and couldn't get it out of the player.

"So for nine hours the tape went on and on, over and over again! He got nine hours of John Gray. Nine hours from Georgia to Florida with a tape that wouldn't turn off! Driving behind, I had no idea that was going on with Doug—and when we got home, after nine hours of listening, I got a sentence and a half out of him. A year ago that would have made me scared. Today, it gave me the greatest laugh!"

6

Greetings from Mars and Venus

The importance of discovering how men and women give and receive love differently is a recurring theme in the success stories of loving couples. Understanding that men are from Mars and women are from Venus has been a key ingredient for immediately improving any relationship. If you were to go to another planet, certainly you would first study its inhabitants' language, culture, and traditions. Without this vital information you would repeatedly and unknowingly offend others and sabotage your relationships. To successfully bring greetings from Mars and Venus and live together in love and peace on earth, we must first understand what our partners truly need.

When you love someone, you naturally treat them in the ways *you* would want to be treated. This loving tendency becomes counterproductive when what we would want is the opposite of what our partners would want. In loving relationships, quite automatically we give our partners what we would want but not necessarily what they want and need. A clear awareness of our differences motivates us to learn about and respect the unique needs of our partners, instead of automatically assuming we know what is best for them.

Without a deeper understanding of how to give and receive love, we continue to be disappointed and frustrated. It's so easy to forget to do the things that matter most to our partners when we instinctively have other needs and priorities. After reading *Men Are from Mars,* men learn the importance of making a woman feel special, cared for, respected, and understood; women learn the importance of trusting, accepting, and appreciating a man. Men learn to focus on doing certain things that say "I care" while women put special emphasis on responding to what a man does in a way that says "I appreciate."

Hearing these stories and examples of couples successfully sharing love not only is inspiring but reminds us once again of the various and different ways we can love our partners.

He Makes Me Feel Special

Debby described a marriage that worked from the beginning. "Before we got married, Spencer talked to my grandma on the phone, and she told him, 'You don't know how special Debby is. You don't know how wonderful—' And Spencer interrupted her to say, 'Grandma, I'm going to treat her like a queen.' And he does. He makes me feel completely special.

"I had been married once before, to someone who was absolutely the wrong partner for me. He was sweet and nice, but we came from totally different ends of the spectrum. We couldn't have been farther apart in every single aspect of our lives. I found out later that people at our wedding were making bets on how long we would stay married. Everyone but me could see what became obvious to me a year into the marriage.

"After the divorce, I was the happiest single person in America. I was just so happy to be *out!* I couldn't find other women who enjoyed being single—they were all miserable, wanting to be married. But I just wanted to date. I was having a great time. The men I met got better and better—I was on a learning curve, and each man I found was more appropriate. But then I started seeing someone who was totally unavailable to me. I liked him and wanted more than I could have. That's when I decided to take out a personal ad.

"Personal ads are a great way to meet people: you say what you want, you're totally in control, and you can really articulate what you're looking for. I knew what I wanted: a date every Saturday night and Sunday afternoon and New Year's Eve, and somebody who could go out with me to weddings, bar mitzvahs, and funerals. Maybe I'd even like to have one weeknight a week in there too.

He told me he was ready for marriage.
He wanted a full-time commitment.

"But when I met Spencer he told me he was ready for marriage. He wanted a full-time commitment. He had been divorced for a year and a half after a thirty-year marriage and wanted to get back to being married. I said nope, I didn't want that. So he told me he'd only stick around a little while, to see if I changed my mind.

"I felt sort of blackmailed by that, but it turned out that I liked having him around. I wanted to see him more than what I'd said about my original requirements. And nowadays it's so cute, because whenever we go to a wedding or a funeral, he's always asking whether he fit the job description and did a good job!

"In fact, I knew pretty soon that this was a man I could marry. In a way I have my parents to thank for that. They had an unhappy marriage and just stayed together 'for the kids.' I begged them to leave each other. When they asked us what we wanted for Christmas we would say, 'Separate!' So from them I learned that I should leave my first husband, that that marriage wasn't going to work. And that's how I knew that this marriage with Spencer was right for me. Things kept *working*. I never knew there could be a marriage like this, because I'd never seen one. But I knew that what was happening was 'right.'

I never knew there could be a marriage like this, because I'd never seen one.

"It's funny. Most people like reading John Gray's work because they have a problem they are trying to fix. But when I came across *Men Are from Mars, Women Are from Venus*, I liked reading it because it affirmed for me that what Spencer and I were doing was actually working. And I saw *why* things worked between us. Even the title made me realize, yes, we come from different planets, it's not *this* man who's different, it's all men. That's just the way it is, so the theme is to accept reality and not try to change it all the time. That kind of acceptance really fit with our temperaments. It's what we thought about, studied in our spiritual lives, practiced. Acceptance of reality was what we were doing.

"Another thing was the tools. Probably the most important communication skill John Gray talks about is listening. And what I have in my husband is a man who just naturally listens. I think I'm extraordinarily lucky to have found him. Suddenly I was being heard, as opposed to being on parallel tracks with a man, not really intersecting. Spencer and I were on the same train. What sums it up is the list he keeps in his wallet of things he wants to buy me in order to please me. He listens so carefully to what I say, not just to him but to other people, that he picks up these little hints and writes them down so he doesn't forget. 'Oh, I saw the cutest thing,' I say. 'This really nice pin in such-and-such a store,' or 'I just love that song.' And he'll write down 'pin in store' or some particular title. He's always regaling me with surprises and notes and special things, I have to be really careful about what I say!

> **He picks up these little hints and writes**
> **them down so he doesn't forget.**

"And he listens to what bothers me too. Now, one thing I've hated is crumbs in the bed. So he bought a whisk broom and has it hanging on his side. He's thoughtful, romantic, and he listens. His actions reflect the fact that he really listens.

"The things we share? Oh, biking, hiking, games. We have a lot of fun and like to laugh a lot. We try to find ways to make each other laugh, and we're both optimists, which helps a lot. One particular thing that bonds us together is the urge to express our gratitude. For example, we started saying grace before dinner, and now it's a chance to say what we're grateful for—not just the food, but each other, where we live, that we have enough money to give some to people who need help. And once a week we do volunteer work, serving in a free dining room and doing other things to give back to the community. We see this as a joyful commitment that we can do together. It's a matter of luck, in a way, that we can take time out to do this, and it helps us bond further, because we have this experience we share. Oh, yes, I count my blessings every day.

"I have no idea what our future is going to

look like. Spencer is nearly twenty years older than me, and he's winding down on his career while my career is just peaking. He sees more leisure time coming up than I do. That's something that's going to come up from time to time, I'm sure, and yet I do look to the future with confidence. I don't know what we'll be doing in fifteen years, but I'm sure we'll be doing it together.

"It just makes me gush with gratitude knowing that Spencer loves me so much. He goes to great lengths to do nice things for me, and each time he does I know he cares about making me happy. This makes me careful not to ask for too much, but just knowing he cares inspires such comfort in me. I do think it comes naturally to women to express gratitude, as John Gray says, and I'm glad John is teaching that skill to people.

Knowing he cares inspires such comfort in me.

"I count my blessings every single day, but the thing I'm most grateful for, I think, is that Spencer listens.

"Not to mention the fact that I have a date every Saturday, Sunday, and New Year's Eve!"

We Couldn't Stop Fighting

Sheri shared, "My husband, Dave, and I were seeing a marriage counselor—not because we didn't love each other, but because we couldn't quit fighting. The stupid thing was, we fought about nothing important. It was mostly just a lot of bickering caused by poor communication. Since I hold a master's degree in counseling, this is somewhat difficult for me to reveal. After all, I should know better. Right? Wrong! It's that old story about the doctor who treats himself having a fool for a doctor.

"Well, I couldn't heal us either, and that's why we were in counseling. As an assignment one week, our therapist told us to read your book. After I started, I couldn't wait to begin discussing it. Soon we began referencing the book as we communicated with each other.

"It wasn't uncommon for us to say such things as 'I guess you're in your cave; let me know when you come out,' or 'I'm okay, I'm just in my cave,' or 'Go ahead and talk; I know it's a Venus thing.' It was amazing how much smoother our lives became. With just a little bit of insight into how each of us functions, we were suddenly able to prevent most of the old arguments. And we were able to leave counseling.

> **"I guess you're in your cave; let me know
> when you come out."**

"Last summer, my employer held a meeting in Puerto Rico. I was required to attend, and my husband was invited. Our first day on the island, we took a water taxi over to a private island for 'fun in the sun.' As we were getting off the water taxi, we met up with a couple of my co-workers and their mates, so we all set off together to explore the island. I should say, we all set off together except Dave.

"My husband just wandered off on his own. He pulled out in front of the group and took off on a different path. For just a moment I considered following after him and giving him a piece of my mind. 'How rude of you to just wander off and leave me. My friends might think you don't want to be with them, or me. You have really embarrassed me, etc.'

"But I stopped myself. Suddenly I realized that he had 'gone into his cave,' and it was okay for him to be off on his own. He was perhaps a bit overwhelmed by the entire experience and just needed to be in his cave for a while to adjust. The best part was that I knew if I just left him alone, when he came back he would be better for having gone off. He would be on his best behavior and I would be even more proud of him as I showed him off to my colleagues.

> I realized that he had "gone into his cave," and it was okay for him to be off on his own.

"As I walked on with my friends, I started to talk about *Men Are from Mars* and how it had changed our lives. One of the guys commented that I was smart to let Dave just go off on his own and that it was probably what he needed to do. I just nodded knowingly, and felt sort of smug because I realized that as a Martian he too understood what I finally understood. I understood because I learned it from the book. He knew it because he was a man. This one simple act of trust, faith, letting go, insight—call it whatever you wish—made all the difference on our trip. Dave came back eventually and joined the group. The rest of the trip was like being on Fantasy Island. We didn't even fight!

> One of the guys commented that I was smart to let my husband just go off on his own.

"Today we still refer to the book. It has become a part of our everyday language. By now our friends have also read it, so we all make references to it on a routine basis. Just last weekend my best friend and I went on an all-day shopping trip. As we were planning it, Dave said to me, 'You girls need to have your time together. It's all about that Venus stuff. Go ahead, stay out as long as you want. I'll be home when you get back.' No woman could ask for more than that!"

Sex and Affection

Alice spoke about her improved sex life. "My husband, Andrew, is the strong, silent type. He has great difficulty showing his feelings. This used to be very hard on me because I didn't feel loved or connected to him. After a while I didn't even want to have sex with him. I need lots of affection in order to become aroused and ready to give myself sexually. I also need reassurances about my attractiveness. Without understanding silent Martians I felt hopeless.

"After reading *Mars and Venus in the Bedroom*, though, I discovered that I could get all the love and attention I needed. I learned that he has all the affection I crave, but it's on the other side of the mountain. That mountain is the sexual sharing of our love.

"I see it all now as a wonderful adventure, a journey in which I need to forgo some of my needs until we get over the mountain. Then, sure enough, after sex my husband is sweet, warm, and affectionate. He is like a different man! He will even say endearing things, such as 'You are a great lover!' or 'You are so beautiful.' He holds me and rubs my back, and often he will open up and talk to me as we lie in each other's arms.

He holds me and rubs my back, and often he
will open up and talk to me as we
lie in each other's arms.

"All of these things I need to remember, storing them in my imaginary 'backpack' so I can be aroused for that next trip up over the mountain!

"For variety, which we women love (I learned that in the book too!), I sometimes see my husband as locked in a big golden cage. Our lovemaking is the key he needs to become freed. It works!

"Yes! I am a willing sexual partner now that I've learned how our needs and responses differ."

Finally Finding Love

Victoria related her story. "I am thirty-six years old, and my husband, Edward, is forty-six. He is my second husband; I am his third wife. Although we have had many painful experiences in our relationships, we both are finally finding love.

"I know my ex-husband loved me in his way, but I always came second with him. His friends came first. When I wanted more, he regarded my needs as a nuisance. After seeing a therapist to deal with the problems in our relationship, I soon made the quantum leap of leaving him. I never regretted the step I took, and never looked back.

"When I first met Edward, the last thing on my mind was another relationship. Friends introduced us when he was visiting from South Africa. My guard was up, and anyway, Edward had a girlfriend back in South Africa. Still, we talked on the phone after he returned, and when his relationship with his girlfriend dwindled out, he flew me over to visit him.

"We knew then we didn't quite click. But a year later Edward visited me and everything was different. At that time I was reading *Men Are from Mars* and he had just finished it. Something unexplainable, unbelievable, and inevitable happened to us. We merged like two oceans. We were simply ready, and the timing couldn't have been better. We were inseparable from that moment on.

"I think the fact that we were not initially head over heels in love helped enormously. We took it slow and became friends, building a foundation for a lasting relationship. And we found we had so much in common it was almost frightening. Edward was every woman's dream: real, kind, warm, honest, sensitive and yet tough, caring, gentle, intelligent, responsible, considerate, understanding, attractive, funny, friendly, easygoing . . . the list can go on and on.

> **He treats me with respect as an equal partner.**

"He treats me with respect as an equal partner. We hold each other, give as many hugs as we need, cuddle, talk about anything and everything. We try to share and cherish every moment we have. What works is the fact that we both listen to each other's wishes, wants, and needs.

"One of Edward's wishes is for me to greet him at the door with a warm and 'happy to see you' hug whenever possible. For me, not only is it wonderful to see him at the end of the day or a trip, but his love for me grows even stronger when I remember his wishes instead of ignoring them. So meeting his wishes is as fulfilling for me as for him. Our love for each other is unconditional, and it grows every day.

"You might think that this man sounds too good to be true. But you just have to know him to know he's a very simple, down-to-earth, kind, and gentle fellow who gives a lot of love and attention and receives it back in the same way. Still, I can't say we don't have our moments. Yes, we argue like everyone else. We raise our voices and we may not like each other at that very moment. I go on and on while sometimes he lives in his cave. But we don't stay mad or hold grudges for long, and we try to remember that our love is stronger than any disagreement, so we cool down pretty fast.

"Now after four years of marriage, I am six months pregnant. At a time like this, we pregnant women want to be loved even more, looked after and pampered like never before. And Edward comes through. He strokes my belly and talks to the baby constantly. The other day, he suggested to me that when the baby arrives he would want to move the furniture so it would be easier for him to get to the baby during the night for feedings. I know he will be a wonderful father. He doesn't mind cleaning, washing dishes, changing diapers. . . . Even though I feel nervous about becoming a mother, Edward makes me feel that it will all be all right.

**We pregnant women want to be loved even
more, looked after and pampered
like never before.**

"We are very blessed to have found each other and the kind of happiness and love neither of us had had. As the proverb suggests, 'One who does not look, does not find.' But it must always be with an open mind, eyes, and ears."

A Classic Martian / Venusian Dilemma

Barbara recounts the change in her marriage: "Roger and I were married three years ago. Our life is wonderful, full, and comfortable. But it was not always that way. Before reading *Men Are from Mars, Women Are from Venus,* we constantly felt at odds with each other. I never felt that he truly listened to me, and he felt that I was never satisfied: a classic Martian/Venusian dilemma.

"I would manufacture upsets in our relationship just to get him to sit and talk with me. Sometimes those conversations would stretch deep into the night, until two or three in the morning. Finally I realized that I was looking for reasons to fight just so he would have to discuss things with me. This gave me his undivided attention. But I also got what I hadn't counted on . . . his anger.

I would manufacture upsets in our relationship just to get him to sit and talk with me.

"Eventually I learned that it was futile to start an argument over an insignificant event, because he would withdraw even further into his cave after the discussions were over. I would feel good, because I'd finally had a chance to talk, spewing out all the things that were on my mind, but it left him frustrated.

"Roger felt responsible for all the feelings I had, and hence he wanted to fix me. I wasn't looking to be fixed; I just wanted him to listen. Since we had this classic 'fix/just listen' routine going, nothing was accomplished in these argument sessions.

"This pattern lasted three years, until I read *Men Are from Mars, Women Are from Venus* and understood the difference between the two of us. I asked Roger to listen to the audiotape and watch the video, and after that we began to relate to each other differently. We began to accept the fact that we were different.

"Now, when I feel he is stubbornly positioned in his Martian mode, I take my index and middle finger, form them into a V, and hold them up behind my head so they show over the top of my hair. I may wiggle them a little and jokingly comment that he is being 'my favorite Martian' again.

**I jokingly comment that he is being
"my favorite Martian" again.**

"We can laugh and joke now about situations that used to initiate an argument, and our relationship has dramatically improved. I understand now that a Martian needs his space, that his cave is off-limits to Venusians, and that he will come out eventually when he's ready. And he understands that a Venusian needs to talk (and talk and talk), and that he, as her favorite Martian, needs to listen and not try to fix her.

"We accept that it's okay to think differently about money, children, sex, work, spending time together, and so on. If we can remember to accept the fact that we're different, we can understand that the other is not being obstinate, stubborn, or disagreeable, but is just from another planet.

We understand that the other is not being obstinate, stubborn, or disagreeable, but is just from another planet.

"For instance, at Christmas, Roger waits to the last minute to buy presents. I like to plan in advance. This used to create a lot of friction. I would try to change him and he would resist. Now I let him be a Martian and am amazed at how much shopping he can do when he is backed up to the wall.

"He used to expect me to be excited about the various features of his car, stereo, and computer. Now he doesn't take it personally. I am just not interested in all the things he is. We are both happy that we are interested in each other and enjoy doing and sharing other things together.

"Above all the special things we do for each other, the most special is we allow each other to be ourselves. For example, he knows I have to travel to see my grown children and my loved grandson. He hates for me to travel away from him and worries about what might happen to me. Yet he understands why I have to do it and resigns himself to my trips.

"On my side, I know he becomes consumed by his work and when he's obsessed he can't think about me. I find this upsetting at times and feel that I come second. Still, I love and admire his commitment to his work—even though sometimes it drives me crazy. I have learned to understand that eventually he will come back to me. Like a stretched rubber band, he does spring back.

"Communication is one of our best areas. Everybody's heard that saying 'Timing is everything.' It is so much better now that I pick the time when I need to talk with Roger about something. It really works when I allow him to exit his cave before beginning to ask him questions.

"I've also learned firsthand that it is plain foolish to tell Roger what to do. He'll only rebel anyway. Instead I have practiced using 'would' and 'will' to make a request rather than directing or ordering him. It works wonders in our conversations. By asking him to help me, using 'would you consider . . . ?' or 'will you please . . . ?' my chances of receiving a yes have dramatically improved.

"I've realized that he is in his cave when he's doing some of his favorite activities: watching sports on TV, working in the garage, doing math problems on the checkbook or the bills, driving his spaceship around the planet. I've found that what works best during these times is not to demand that he talk to me, but to wait for a commercial, a break in the work, or a stoplight. Then I ask for his opinion or initiate a conversation.

"When Roger and I were married, I thought he would be 'everything' to me. Now, though, I see that it's not my marriage partner's responsibility to be the sole provider of 'everything' in my life. Meeting my needs is my responsibility, just as it's his responsibility to fulfill his needs. Through understanding our natural and inherent differences, it became very apparent that expecting my Roger to be everything to me was a foolish idea. What pressure on his shoulders to expect him to provide it all!

It's not my marriage partner's responsibility to be the sole provider of "everything" in my life.

"Living with someone from a different planet is an ongoing challenge. Every day brings fresh new challenges in ways we relate to each other. Keeping a sense of humor, a sharp memory of our differences, and a commitment not to take life so seriously are the keys to our healthy and happy marriage.

"My wonderful husband has just one contribution to make to this story, and in true Martian fashion it's short and to the point: 'The most important thing to remember,' says Roger, 'is that we're different.'"

Staying Together

Adrian told her love story. "When I think about what Sean and I have been through over our almost twenty years of marriage, I'm sure that many other couples would not have stuck it out. Sean's parents have been married for forty-five years, but mine divorced when I was eleven. That's a fifty-fifty chance of long-term success based on family history. So what does keep us together?

"Let me give you a little history. Sean and I met in college when I was eighteen and he was twenty. I was majoring in special education and he was majoring in theater with a minor in mass communications. We met at the university theater, as I was also interested in acting, and we became friends.

"I believe that that was the first key to our romantic success: we were friends before we were lovers. I confided in Sean and he in me. I dated all his friends and only later learned that he was waiting for me to notice him.

"Prior to the time I fell in love with Sean, I had decided that I was through with men. I felt that men were not to be trusted and only wanted to have sex with me. My young romantic ideas had been dashed by bad experiences. I was actually nineteen when Sean kissed me in front of the whole world, on a busy corner by the dorm. I realized I was in love with him, and it came as a bit of a surprise.

"After that kiss, he was not pushy about getting me into bed, and that made me love him all the more. In fact, I was very clearly the one who invited him to stay one evening quite a while after we were involved. As a lover he was sensitive, romantic, and very sexy. When I was twenty and he was twenty-two we were married.

After that kiss, he was not pushy about getting me into bed, and that made me love him all the more.

"Sean is now forty-two and I am forty. Our children are nearly grown. I am a Montessori teacher and Sean is a theater stage manager, production manager, and freelance writer. Our love has become much deeper and richer over the years. Each challenge we have faced has made us stronger.

"When Sean's theater life kept him away at night for long periods of time, we never would have made it through but for the strong trust we had in each other. I went out with my girlfriends so that I would not pine away at home. In our case, absence made the heart grow fonder. Throughout our life together, we have also had our lives apart. If we were going through a tough time, we would stick it out. We sought the help of a therapist when we had trouble with our son. We read self-help books, talked to friends, recognized the parts we each played, and took the time to work things out. Humor has been an important ingredient in getting through rough spots, as well as the patience and perseverance to keep trying.

"We look at each other today and realize that we love each other more than we did in our younger days. Our sex life has taken on new and exciting realms as we know each other so well. By the same token, there is still a hint of mystery and the realization that no matter how well you know someone, that person may surprise you.

The little things score points with me.

"Sean knows the little things that score points with me. We read the newspaper together and discuss what is going on in the world. When elections come up, we share our opinions on the issues and often we go to vote together. Sean reads stories and poems out loud to me and I love it. We go on walks, scratch each other's backs, and rub each other's feet. We enjoy art, theater, music, movies, museums, hiking, and camping together. We have not traveled nearly as much as we have dreamed about, but when we do take a trip we learn about where we are going together, and often Sean will read stories to me about the places we will go.

"We have always supported each other in our jobs. When Sean wants my opinion, I listen to commercials he has written. I have seen almost every show that he has had a part in. He always comes to the little shows my students put on. Sometimes he is a part of a show, such as the time he read the story while my daughter and I did the shadow puppets for a special presentation during the holidays. He will read and edit my classroom newsletters for me if I ask him to. He has helped clean up the classroom after big events and actively participated in my school's fund-raisers.

"We have learned that the best time to communicate is when we are both rested and not the minute we walk in the door after work or when we are under deadlines, tired, or sick. We give each other the space we need to get things done. I have learned to give Sean his 'cave time.'

"We have gotten better at asking for what we need in a straightforward, nonjudgmental way. It took a while to remember to preface my requests with 'would you?' instead of 'could you?' It's a little thing, but he really appreciates it.

"During times when our jobs have put us in the position of 'ships passing in the night,' we write notes to each other. In this way, we do not get too far behind in what is going on with each other and the children.

"We will be continually learning together with each challenge that life presents. We are soon to be a couple with no children at home. Our daughter is a senior, and this last year before she goes to college is very precious to us. At the same time, we are faced with Sean being unemployed and with all the ups and downs that go with that. I feel that we will get through this also. We have a strong foundation."

Knowing What You Want

Mitzi shared, "At age thirty-eight, I had reached a point where if I wasn't in a really *good* relationship I preferred being by myself. I had had some long-term and some short-term relationships, but by then I could pretty much tell if there was any future to one or another. I really honored my intuition about things and had a strong sense of the qualities I desired in a relationship.

"Those qualities were trust, respect, friendship, warmth, and love. And I had a sense of the type of person I needed to build a relationship with: someone mature, intelligent, willing to make a commitment, consistent, open to continued growth and new ideas, someone healthy, energetic, and with a good sense of humor, someone I could enjoy.

"I felt really *good* about my life at that time, and whoever came into it was going to have to enhance it—we would have to enhance *each other's* lives. This was a special time for me. I was integrating two parts of myself: the emotional and the intellectual. I could look at the different levels of myself and think about a partner who would complement me. We would create a wonderful life together.

I felt really *good* about my life at that time,
and whoever came into it was going
to have to enhance it.

"During that good time, I went to an art opening at a gallery with a close woman friend.

And there I met Frank. He just walked up to us and started talking in a friendly way. I remember thinking after a couple of minutes that he was very insightful, intelligent, thought things out. At this same moment, my friend was excitedly whispering to me, saying, 'This is the perfect guy for you, Mitzi. I got the picture of you two together as he walked up.' But I was surprised and continued to have a conversation with Frank.

"We talked for a bit and then went our own ways, but outside in the street we saw each other again, and I told him I was going to listen to some jazz with my friends. He met me there and after the show said, 'You know, it's a full moon. Would you like to take a walk on the beach?' I was impressed that he knew it was a full moon.

"So we did walk on the beach—and then, when he left, he gave me his name and phone number. 'If you'd like to get together again,' he said, 'please give me a call.' I'd never had *that* happen before. I think Frank had decided that he wasn't interested in going out with someone unless that person was really interested in him. It was really up to me if I wanted to contact him— all of a sudden I felt responsible, like the relationship was in my hands, and what if it didn't go well? It was fascinating having that aspect to the situation.

"But it seemed to me like Frank was a real

person, and I wanted a real person in my life. I decided to take a chance, and I called. We made plans to get together, and we've been together from that point on, over five years now.

"Unknown to me, Frank had taken John Gray's workshop and really enjoyed it. We heard that John was coming to Hawaii and Frank thought I'd enjoy a workshop professionally, as a counselor, and personally too. We attended together, and I think we've assisted at every single one since then. During the first one we had some sort of argument and couldn't get out of it. I said, let's just try one more thing, a John Gray technique, and we switched modalities, from talking to giving hugs. Within a couple of minutes we'd dissolved away the hurt and anger and had gotten to the place where we could respect each other's point of view. Then we got some sleep.

> By giving hugs, within a couple of minutes we'd dissolved away the hurt and anger.

"What was wonderful about our relationship that first year was that we just hibernated and healed—I felt a deep healing just being with him, and the sense that I was home. I had my wounds and fears and questions about finding the right partner, so when we spent that first year together, we relaxed, did little rituals and games together, listened to music, and a lot of old things dissolved away. After that we began to see friends again, and each circle accepted the other, which I thought was a wonderful sign.

"What's exciting to me is that there's been a natural progression in our relationship. We've moved at our own pace toward more commitment, more warmth and love, an ongoing current of energy that I feel more and more. I have a positive faith in the future for us. I trust Frank a lot.

"In previous relationships, maybe I hadn't trusted that the person could handle his life, and I'd wind up being healer, teacher, mother, whatever. But I have a lot of confidence in Frank's competence, his ability to deal with whatever comes up, and that he'll choose the best way. I've learned that to love a man is to trust and accept him. Through learning to trust and allowing him to be himself, I have been able to find a deeper acceptance. I know he appreciates that a lot.

"It's a real luxury just to be able to be yourself and connect that way with another person. Ultimately it would be great if everyone could feel that way, but one thing or another keeps people from really revealing themselves and showing themselves to the other person. It's wonderful when you can just come across as who you are and know that you're okay and you'll be accepted.

"Besides an increasing acceptance, through participating in John's seminars we have found a common language, a framework, we can use to think about our relationship that isn't difficult, confusing, or abstract. It's very understandable, and the information we've gotten can be put into use and practice immediately.

**We have found a common language,
a framework, we can use to think about
our relationship that isn't difficult,
confusing, or abstract.**

"I've looked back over my past relationships when I started really thinking about 'what men want,' and I could see that, even with the best intentions and trying to do the right thing, I did cause some damage in those relationships. From John Gray I got a clearer idea of what men and women needed and what was important to them in a relationship. Believe me, I integrated that information into my profession as well as my personal life. To build on the things that work, to do the things that work in relationships—*that's* what we've done.

"There was a kind of a natural flow to what happened between Frank and me, and I didn't feel the need to push and manipulate things. I had the trust that the right things would unfold at the right times. And they have."

Overcoming the Fear of Commitment

Frank told the story from his point of view. "I was married when I was twenty-one; the lady was seventeen. She was from Australia, and part of her agenda was to marry to stay in the country. I felt pushed into the marriage: it didn't feel right, I didn't want to do it, but I didn't have enough self-confidence to assert my own way. And the marriage was a real disaster. When our daughter was three weeks old, I discovered that my wife was having an affair with my best friend. It was a horrible ordeal, and the marriage was irretrievable.

"After that I made up my mind that I was never going to be forced into marriage, *never.*

I made up my mind that I was never going to be forced into marriage.

"Throughout my twenties and thirties I had a very varied love life—lonely sometimes, then dating very attractive women, then falling in love. In my midthirties, I lived with a very exciting French gal with all the knowledge of how to do a love affair, with candles and incense and beautiful music by Bach. It was very exciting, she was a very exciting person. And then at dinner one night she asked me, 'Can't we get married?' The fork stuck halfway between my plate and my mouth. It seemed reasonable, she was a terrific woman, but I remembered my dictum that I'd never be forced into marriage. And that was the end of a great relationship.

"About a year later, after dating around, I met a gal who was very attractive to me. We began living together and it was a good, solid relationship. She was helping me raise my daughter. And then, on a romantic vacation to San Francisco, she put to me the same proposition. We needed to get married or she would move on. It was a biological-clock kind of thing. This was very painful, because I loved her and I loved her family. But I had to stick with my central belief. We split up.

"For a time I decided, I'm going to have a wild time. I knew I didn't want to be married—maybe because I had a desire for other women—but I didn't want to be unfaithful either. So I decided to take a year and a half off from my business and enjoy life. And I did—I had a heck of a good time, one of my most fun years with my friends. I went out with lots and lots of extremely beautiful women.

"Would you believe it? It ended painfully. I had a beautiful young German girlfriend—and one day she announced that she was absolutely in love with my best friend. It was like a mirror image, an echo, of my first marriage. I didn't know what to do. All my theories had finally been used up.

"A little while later I went to an opening at an art gallery, and there I met Mitzi. We had a friendly conversation, and after a while we decided to go and get a cup of coffee. We went to an espresso place where she was meeting some friends. I thought, Here is a warm, loving, nice person.

"At the espresso house, Mitzi brought out some photos of herself taken at Halloween. For the opening she was wearing a long dress, but in the pictures she had on a string bikini, and this kind of clamshell bra. I saw that she had an incredible body, and all of a sudden I felt a big surge of attraction toward her. That wasn't her intent, I don't think, but I went, Wow! This is a very attractive person. I hate to admit it, but for me that was the initial hook.

"We went down to the beach and kissed a while, and then I gave her my number. 'If you want to get together, give me a call,' I said. I left it in her hands. In a couple of days she called, and I found out I was very attracted to her in all senses. Look, I was heading toward forty, I realized I was going to die someday, and I didn't want to be some single guy running around trying to get laid all the time.

I realized I was going to die someday, and I didn't want to be some single guy running around trying to get laid all the time.

"And Mitzi made things easy. She had a really nice home, not fancy in any respect, but she made it very comfortable with all the things she loved up on the walls. And she was into health foods, as I was. She knew how to make things beautiful. I liked coming back from the salt mines, my contracting business, to lighted candles all around the house, heavenly music, and a person interested in everything I was doing. Oh, she had her own stories to tell too. She just had that nesting thing down naturally. Also, she had real spiritual beliefs, which she was sincere about. It meant our relationship had the possibility to go further than just, 'What's for dinner? How much money did you make this year?' Spiritual development—that was one of my hidden agendas in searching for a relationship.

"I liked it that Mitzi was in a business that helped people. She was *always* helping people, and they were always calling her. Also, it was quite unusual, but she really had no desire to have kids. She loved kids, played with kids, but didn't seem to want to have one of her own. That wasn't a driving force for me either, since I already have a child I am close to and love very much.

"Especially after I introduced her to the seminars, we constantly employed John Gray's techniques to smooth things over so they didn't get blown up. It helps a lot to remember that we are different and there is nothing wrong with our different ways of looking at things. It also helped me to figure out what she really needed and then honor her by respecting what was important to her.

"I like that Mitzi is very feminine. One thing John said that scared me was that as men get older, they naturally become more feminine and that they must be careful to stay grounded in their masculinity. That's okay with me but he also said women tend to become more masculine and need to stay connected to their femininity. I told her, 'It scares me to think that you might eventually become a growly old man. Let's work to make sure that doesn't happen.' It's a matter of working on things and nurturing her feminine needs.

> "It scares me to think that you might eventually become a growly old man."

"But I still had my old agenda. The first week we got together, I told her, 'Don't expect me to get married. I don't really believe in it.' And that was no problem with her. We never even discussed getting married after that.

"Fast-forward now to the point where we had been living together for five years. We had gone camping in a very remote valley on Kauai. I remember it was my birthday, August 20. I woke up with no *idea* of what was about to transpire. We had planned to go on a hike with some old hippies called the 'Outlaws' we had met.

"We wound up in the most beautiful place I'd ever seen: a series of waterfalls with a slippery slide, it must have been like the original Garden of Eden. Mitzi and I went to the very highest of waterfalls and got in the water together with the sun shining on us and water falling down around us. And suddenly a crazy thought, with no prior warning, entered my mind: I should ask Mitzi to marry me.

"I'm totally nonpressured; I'm with the person I love so much; this is my birthday and the most beautiful place on earth.

"But the words wouldn't come out. I finally managed to ask her after three or four minutes of choking.

"'What?' she asked, and I had to say it again.

"'Of course,' said Mitzi.

"Since then we haven't talked about it much, but we sent out a Christmas letter saying we were engaged. I feel good about it, having made a decision like that without pressure. There's an inevitability that we'll be together forever."

Learning to Open Up

Kyle shared, "About three years ago a friend of mine called me and said, 'You gotta hear this guy. His name is John Gray. I know you and Gary have been going to couple's counseling and I really think you two would benefit. . . .' She was exploding with excitement and proceeded to tell me how this information was different from other things she had heard. *Men Are from Mars, Women Are from Venus*—the title of this book piqued my interest, so with much effort I talked my husband, Gary, into joining me at a seminar. He said, 'If this is another one of those male-bashing events, I'm going to leave.'

"If this is another one of those male-bashing events, I'm going to leave."

"We were both open and eager to learn, but as John proceeded to say how women needed to be cared for, I was perplexed. At that time, I didn't know the power of being cared for as a woman, so I challenged John. 'We can take care of ourselves! We're more than capable. We can do anything a man can do!' I cried, mustering up a lot of support from other women there. I could hear their faint cheers.

"John was gentle with me. He asked me to turn around and share my shirt with the audience: 'Bitch, bitch, bitch,' it read in black letters across my chest. The audience roared with laughter. Then John explained, helping me tap into an important piece of the puzzle I was obviously ready to find. He told me that a part of my femininity was suppressed, so I could not allow myself to be cared for. I didn't realize how much resentment I was carrying around in my bag of hurts—my father had abused me physically and emotionally as a child, and being uncherished and uncared-for by my father led me to develop strong masculine survival skills. I was out of balance.

"Watching my mother be abused as well solidified my behavior. As an adult, because of my beliefs, I had taken on some of my husband's job description in the relationship. And therefore his needs weren't getting met. He felt less of a man, while I believed—subconsciously—that I had to strip men of their power so I wouldn't get hurt anymore. All this was based in fear, and love can't come from fear. John helped me unlock the key to those feelings, and after attending a series of lectures and workshops and reading John's book and listening to his tapes, I started to transform.

"Being cared for is a magnificent gift for the female side of me. It has been a healing experience for my soul. My husband does things for me now that I can really show him I appreciate, and the more I show my appreciation, the more he wants to do. He 'toils' for me now, and instead of feeling uncomfortable—feeling I should do everything and have no vulnerability—I find I really feel loved when I am cared for. The key is that I had to allow this to take place, learn to trust and let my defenses down.

> Instead of feeling uncomfortable—feeling
> I should do everything and have no
> vulnerability—I found I really feel loved
> when I am cared for.

"The result of learning to trust my husband was that I started to blossom. And by learning to trust him, I saw how he blossomed. By encouraging him I found that he had leaped to new heights, and I started to admire him more and more. He began to validate and reassure me, and my self-esteem started to soar. I was recapturing that female part of me and bathing in it as if it were warm sunshine—I had no idea I could feel so wonderful. All the primary needs John taught us have helped us both grow in love. I discovered that there was no conspiracy to keep women down and controlled. It was just that men and women have different needs. We just have to find the willingness to discover and then honor those differences.

> I discovered that there was no conspiracy to
> keep women down and controlled.

"While I have learned to give Gary his 'cave time,' Gary learned from John to listen to me without giving me a solution. He has told me that this was the hardest part for him: his job was to give answers, so when he was first learning to just listen he would actually put his hand tightly over his mouth. This was really painful for him, though I found it funny. We practiced, Gary learned, and now when I go into my deepest, darkest place, called the well, Gary listens and comforts me. With his support and his knowledge of what I need, I come back up to the top extremely fast, loving and appreciating him more than ever because he listened.

"I have not only a better understanding of men but a better understanding of myself. Letting down my barriers and letting Gary in so that I can receive his love and share mine has been an enormous gift. It is a great pleasure for me to share the enlightening experiences I've had on my journey with John's work."

Starting Over

Robert's story reminds us to appreciate what we have. "I met Doreen at a barbecue at my house in 1991. I had been divorced and single for about ten years. I was fifty-three and ready to find a mate to share my accomplishments, to share the sunrises and sunsets with. Doreen had been married for thirty-five years in a marriage she described as terrible, *hor*rible. She'd been divorced about a year when we met. 'I'm not ready for a relationship yet,' she said.

"Fine. I'm a patient person.

"Within three weeks from that barbecue, we were living together. Not very long after that, we were married.

"Our relationship had no hidden agendas, no need for support. It was one of total giving. As far as material things were concerned, we had two of everything—houses, cars, furniture sets. Our agenda was to enjoy each other, our life, and our golden years. And we were financially comfortable. We were able to do it.

"I worked at a power plant and she as a patient advocate at a test site. We were both professionals, professional negotiators. Doreen was a nurse-practitioner, a very intelligent lady, and a leader. Very quickly we had the bright idea to drop out of our commuter van pools and travel back and forth to work together. She'd drop me off at the plant in the morning and pick me up in the afternoon. It was super, because we could talk and chat together. I could see her Jeep coming down the road and visualize her bouncing up and down. It was really great.

"'Have you ever been to the opera?' asked Doreen shortly after we were married. 'Nope, but

I'm willing,' I answered. 'You've made my life!' she cried. 'I've never been able to find anyone to go with me.' The first opera we saw was *The Marriage of Figaro*. I was hooked: I went out and bought two tuxedos. And let me tell you as an aside that after Doreen died, the San Diego Opera Company dedicated a performance of *Macbeth* to her, their loyal fan.

"When Doreen wanted something or wanted to do something, I could never say no to the lady. If it was in my power physically, mentally, or financially, we'd get it. And I know why: because I had her such a short time. It was only three years, but if someone had told me it was going to be three days, three hours, three seconds, I would have taken it, because it was true love. I think the reason was that we were mature. We knew what we wanted, and that was to share. In her own marriage her ex would say they couldn't afford this or that, so she went on vacations all on her own. For myself, it was the same way; everything I did I did alone.

> It was only three years, but if someone had told me it was going to be three days, three hours, three seconds, I would have taken it, because it was true love.

"So we started to travel. We had wonderful, wonderful trips—to Fiji, New Zealand, Australia, Cabo San Lucas. And closer to home we began searching for a place where we could live. Doreen didn't want to live in California anymore, so we bought an RV and took off—Arizona, New Mexico, Colorado . . . we went everywhere. And then one day I remembered a place I'd been: Cedar City, Utah. We took the RV up there and it was wonderful. There was a Shakespeare festival— Doreen fell in love with the place. As we were driving down the highway, suddenly Doreen said, 'What's that?' Up on the hill was an unfinished three-story log cabin. We had a realtor look into it and found out the owner was desperate. We offered him $80,000, and that was that. We had it.

"In June Doreen's house in California sold. In July my house sold. In August we closed the property in Cedar City, hired a contractor, and made that place into a fabulous place—the only house in Utah with a bidet.

"On September 14 Doreen was diagnosed with dermatital polymyelitis.

"On December 11, never having seen our finished home, Doreen died.

"It seemed like a cruel joke to me. I lost my total agenda, because my agenda was Doreen. I lost all sense of mission, of meaning. Doreen's funeral was on December 16; on December 21 the movers came to move me into the house. From her death until about July, I watched the O. J. Simpson trial, and that was the whole of my day. I gained forty pounds, five inches on my waist. I had no desire to do anything. My only companion was our cat, Bobby—a wonderful friend to me. But I was completely devastated. Doreen and I were set to play and I had lost my playmate.

"What helped me was a bereavement support group I heard about on the radio. I attended twice a week and learned there that it was all right to grieve, to cry, to *feel*. I didn't know how to grieve at all. I learned in the group that it was okay to be angry, to talk to Doreen at her favorite tree, to get into her Jeep and cry, even to write her letters. It hurt to do these things, but it was wonderful just to be able to feel.

"The grieving, I think, was a very cleansing experience. For a year I was like a hermit on a mountain—three and a half miles from town on twenty acres, all alone. I let the grief wash over me like a huge wave. I had no distractions, no people to deal with. I did my grieving and was healed.

I let the grief wash over me like a huge wave.

"And then, with Bobby's companionship and the support of the group, I was ready to move on and open my life up again. I sold the house and moved to Eugene, and I didn't look back. I met a lady there, and since then the grief and mourning have ebbed, though Doreen still lives in my heart.

"It was after Doreen's death that I picked up *Men Are from Mars, Women Are from Venus* and *Mars and Venus in the Bedroom.* About five months after her death, I was able to concentrate and read them. And I saw us in the books. Totally. In fact, she would actually use some of the terms Dr. Gray used, like 'walking on eggs.' I saw her wave cycles. I could remember when I would go into my cave. And I knew I'd been a problem solver, a Martian with a spear and sword and shield, here to solve all your problems, fair damsel—oh, weak one. But Doreen was not weak, and as I read the book I thought, Gee, there are things I understand now.

"Doreen always told me I was the only man who *listened* to her, so I found out I was doing something right. But sometimes we'd be going along with some nice warm fuzzy pillow talk, and all of a sudden it would turn into winter in Antarctica. And I'd wonder, What happened?

"It was because my Martian ego was there saying, I'll fix it, don't worry. That didn't work, and the book cleared it up for me. I could see from the book that it wasn't selfishness on either of our parts; it was just that we were ignorant of the intimate art of listening. Instead of hearing your mate, you listen. That's what the book showed me.

"The book and the words are a very strong solvent. They clear away, wash away, any type of ego façade—and also dissolve the feeling that it's wrong to feel. For me, they reinforced my new knowledge that in bereavement whatever I was feeling was all right. When you lose your mate, you feel you're no longer needed or cherished. And that's exactly what I felt: the lack of being needed. I recognize that now.

"In my new relationship, the things I learned from Dr. Gray function wonderfully. Mostly it's the science of listening. My new friend recognizes that as a value; she just wants to be listened to. 'I'm so tired. I have a cold. It's been a hard day.' I suppress the Mr. Fix-it syndrome and just listen. And when she looks at me and says, 'Bob, you're so incredibly understanding,' I'm saying under my breath, 'Both of us thank you, Dr. Gray.'"

A footnote: This year I married the nice lady I described above. In our home we have two books to live by: the Bible and *Men Are from Mars, Women Are from Venus.*

7

Mars and Venus Together Forever

Love can last a lifetime, but it requires the ability to continually let go of our expectations about how our partners should be and behave and to find a greater understanding and acceptance. The acceptance that we are from different planets frees us to connect without having to change each other. This new understanding helps us to make sense of why our partner doesn't think and feel the way we do.

But there are some things that happen in a relationship that are not acceptable; some behaviors need to be changed for love to thrive. To be forgiving does not mean to accept or embrace abuse. To be loving we must also set boundaries and limits.

> To be forgiving does not mean to accept or
> embrace abuse.

Some behaviors—like violence, addiction problems, lying, and infidelity—are clearly unacceptable. We need to say, "This is unacceptable and I need you to clearly acknowledge your mistake and promise never to do it again. I feel that before I can open up again to trust your commitment not to do it again, you need or we need to seek professional help." If your partner is unwilling to acknowledge his or her mistake or the need to get help, then in most cases the only loving answer is to let your partner be responsible for correcting himself or herself and temporarily separate.

Saying no to unsupportive behavior may feel mean because you "mean" what you say, but it is not an act of love to allow someone to repeatedly hurt you. Sometimes our greatest challenge in a relationship is to set that boundary in a loving way and with forgiveness.

Everyone makes mistakes. To forgive those mistakes is the action of love. To forgive strengthens our love. Without forgiveness we cannot grow in love. In a sense it exercises our love and makes it stronger. To not forgive can be as hurtful to ourselves as the perpetrator's original mistake was. When we do not forgive, we hold on to our hurt and we hold the other in a place of being unable to change.

To not forgive is just as hurtful to ourselves as the perpetrator's original mistake was.

To forgive is to let go of our pain. It is also to let go of trying to change the person. Sometimes we passively endure abuse hoping that if we just love the person he or she will change. This submissive nonresistance is not forgiveness and generally doesn't help. It only makes matters worse. The challenge and responsibility of the "victim" is to first protect oneself from being hurt again and then to wish the other person well. We must try to see our partners as capable of eventually changing without our direct help.

In my seminars I focus on all the little things, all the little mistakes that couples make because they really don't understand each other. These little mistakes are easy to forgive, both because they are little and also because it's clear that they arise out of our partners' ignorance. They don't know better, they are from a different planet. Couples laugh together at their mistakes.

Although I don't directly deal with a lot of

the big mistakes in my seminars, couples write to me and share how that environment "miraculously" helped them to forgive their partners and themselves for the big mistakes. By learning to forgive the little mistakes, they were able to forgive the big mistakes.

By learning to forgive the little mistakes, couples were able to forgive the big mistakes

---

When we focus on forgiving what is easiest, then gradually our ability to forgive is strengthened so that we are capable of forgiving the big ones. If you have a heavy load to carry and you are out of shape, the best solution is to start by carrying the smallest and easiest pieces until you build up your strength. Then carry the heaviest pieces. Similarly, in a relationship, start with the little issues; then, the big issues stop being so big or difficult to handle.

Forgiveness and Apologies

Equally important to finding forgiveness is the ability to apologize. Forgiveness and taking responsibility to correct behavior are the two wings of love. Just as it takes time to forgive, it takes time to correct a behavior. Whenever there is a crisis in a relationship there are always two polarities working. The person who committed the mistake needs to look at it, and the other partner needs to look at forgiving. The wound heals most effectively when both participate in the healing process.

It is hard to forgive if your partner does not apologize and work toward correcting the mistake; and it is hard to apologize and work toward correction if your partner does not forgive. It is unrealistic to assume that your partner will never make mistakes, just as it is unrealistic to assume that everything is easily forgiven. It is not. Sometimes forgiveness takes months—even years.

To love is the willful intention to serve your partner according to his or her wishes and an openness to receive your partner's support when it serves your needs. To forgive is to acknowledge that you still wish to serve your partner and that you are still open to receiving his or her support in some way if it serves your needs. When we have been open to our partners' support and it does not come, then we begin to close down. We may wish them well, but it takes more time before we can open up to receive their support again.

> To forgive is to acknowledge that you
> still have goodwill and you are open
> to receiving support.

To apologize is to say that you understand and validate your partner's response and acknowledge that you made a mistake that you intend to correct. An apology acknowledges unconditional responsibility for your mistake and a commitment to do something about it.

> An apology acknowledges unconditional
> responsibility for your mistake and a
> commitment to do something about it.

In correcting your behavior, you are sharpening your ability to give and receive love. In forgiving a mistake, you are also creating the opportunity to open up and again give and receive love. In this way, forgiveness and responsibility go hand in hand.

Unhealthy Relationships

In an unhealthy relationship, it is usually clear which person is responsible—particularly when big mistakes are involved. There is generally a good guy and a bad guy. When this is the case, separation is the only answer. In such cases, the victim's only fault was picking this person to be with; nevertheless, he or she still has a responsibility to find forgiveness.

While the victim takes time to focus on finding forgiveness, the partner focuses on finding the resolve and assistance to solve his or her own problem. It is only after time has passed and healing has taken place that a couple can begin to examine whether it is appropriate to reconcile.

How do you know if you should try again? No one can answer that question for you; you must listen to your loving heart. After healing, sometimes the answer is, "I love this person, I forgive this person, they have changed but I don't want to be married to them." For others, a different answer emerges: "I love this person, I forgive them, they have changed and I want to be married to them."

Healthier Relationships

As we become healthier and more responsible in our lives, the line between victim and perpetrator is not so clear. Even though a relationship is healthier, our partners can still make big mistakes.

For example, when a woman has an affair, a man can look to how his own behavior has been a part of that process. Although she clearly has made a big mistake (having the affair or lying), his neglect of her played a part.

Particularly with a new understanding of how men and women are different, he can see how in many small ways he contributed to the infidelity. It is not so clear-cut who is at fault. When this is the case, the healing can occur more quickly and couples generally get back together.

> In healthier relationships, it is not so clear-cut who is at fault.

When a man is the victim, he needs to first withdraw and look at his feelings; but then he has to focus primarily on what part he played. As he gains more objectivity and a sense of responsibility, his ability to forgive will increase.

This process is what happens when men begin to understand that men are from Mars and women are from Venus. A man may feel hurt but as he hears one example after another of the mistakes all men make, he begins to lighten up and see how he contributed to the problem. This increasing objectivity helps him to forgive his partner. The more he can see his side of the problem, the easier it is to fully forgive.

When a woman is the victim, it is the other way around. If she first has the opportunity to share her feelings about what happened, then she is able to gain more objectivity and see more clearly her part in the problem. The most effective way for her to find forgiveness is first to share all her feelings, and then receive an apology; at that point, after sharing more feelings, she is able to see more clearly how she contributed to the problem as well. Generally when she can see that her contribution to the problem is greater than just innocently picking the wrong person, she will open up to her partner and the couple can come back together and experience greater love than before.

It is important not to push a woman into looking at her part of the problem first. This would have the effect of minimizing or invalidating her feelings of being neglected. It is vital that she first be able to feel what she feels. After that, an objectivity can be gained that is also warm, loving, and forgiving.

It is vital that a woman first feel what she feels. After that, an objectivity can be gained that is also warm, loving, and forgiving.

When women understand that men are from Mars and women are from Venus, they experience greater forgiveness because they first hear that their feelings are valid. Then they are open to begin seeing how it is not just their husbands that make certain mistakes, but most men. After that, they begin to open up and hear all the mistakes that women commonly make. With this greater objectivity, a woman is able to see her part in the problem and forgiveness is much greater.

How Men Heal

Generally speaking, men and women heal from wounds differently. Women usually need to talk more about their feelings, while men need some time to withdraw before they can, eventually, talk about their feelings. What opens a man up the most is the feeling that he is not a victim and that to some degree he can solve the problem. A man's greatest challenge is to take responsibility for his contribution to a problem.

....

**A man's greatest challenge is to take
responsibility for his contribution
to a problem.**

....

Whenever a man feels responsible, at least to some degree, he feels the power to change a situation. When a man is hurt, he first needs to pull away; after some time, having gained greater objectivity, he can see his part in the problem or see how he can solve the problem. With this awareness, his loving feelings can return.

Sometimes to find that objectivity he may need to temporarily back off from the problem (take a vacation, wander aimlessly, or bury himself in work). In other situations, he may find a therapist and express his feelings through talking. If he can express and understand his feelings *and* see his part of the problem, then he can come back to feeling his love and forgiveness.

How Women Heal

Women go through this same process but in a different order. To find forgiveness in her heart, a woman first needs to feel that her feelings are heard, understood, and validated. Having found forgiveness, she is able to back up and recognize more clearly her part of the problem. A woman's greatest challenge is to let go of her resentments and find forgiveness.

A woman's greatest challenge is to let go of her resentments and find forgiveness.

This process of communicating is ideally done in the presence of a trained marriage counselor. What a man needs to know is that no matter how authentic his remorse is, his wife will feel safer sharing her feelings in the presence of someone else. His willingness to seek help or see a counselor is in itself healing, for it acknowledges and validates her need for extra support to open up. In this safe situation, she will be able to share her feelings more deeply and the process will be more effective.

The Healing Crisis

One of the most painful and challenging experiences in a marriage is infidelity. Yet, I have witnessed hundreds of couples heal the pain of betrayal and rebuild trust. With the assistance of counseling, they were able to find the forgiveness and change necessary to start over together, rather than stagnating in resentment.

The length of time required to heal the hurt of betrayal tends to go hand in hand with how long the mistake was made. For example, if a man was having an affair for a long time, then the healing will take more time.

> **The length of time required to heal a hurt tends to go hand in hand with how long the mistake was made.**

Taking the necessary time to forgive and heal can result in a much better relationship. The crisis of an affair can bring up such strong feelings and emotions that when they are expressed and heard, an enormous amount of love surfaces and couples fall in love again. Suddenly their love is more earnest; having survived the crisis, their love is somehow more real, meaningful, and deep.

Having passed a test, they have touched and felt true love, which is lasting and forever.

> **Having survived the crisis of an affair, love is somehow more real, meaningful, and deep; it is truly lasting and forever.**

To hear these stories of healing automatically uplifts our spirits, for it reminds us of the enormous power of love. It gives hope and helps us to appreciate what we have. When one person takes a step to open his or her heart, it moves us all toward greater love. Let's look at just a few of the hundreds of stories I have heard from couples who have found forgiveness after infidelity and continued to grow together in love.

Lisa and Steven

Lisa told her story. "Steven and I lived together for a long time—we had been together for about eight years—but we were both afraid to make the commitment to get married. Why? Well, both of us were afraid of failure, I think. I had come from a family where all my brothers and sisters had married and then gotten divorced. And Steven had been married once before, when he was much younger. It seemed safer to both of us just to go on living together rather than risking failure, and to make that scary commitment to 'forever.'

"But we started doing John Gray's seminars and listening to his tapes—and this feeling came over us that possibly we could make it, that we would have some tools to use when things got rough. We were still afraid, but we were talking about it, moving in on it. Then we actually agreed and set a date for our wedding. What I didn't know was that Steve was more afraid than I was.

"'There's something we need to talk about,' he said to me one day. He was actually in tears, and I knew that whatever it was was really big. My mind was racing—I thought someone had died.

"'Look, I've done something really terrible, Lisa,' he said. And he told me he had had an affair.

"He was completely remorseful, took 100 percent responsibility for what he'd done. It was absolutely clear he felt horrible about it. And he told me, 'I don't know what to do about it.'

"I was totally shocked. On some level I had felt the distance, but I hadn't been sure what it was all about. As I looked back, I saw that I had known that something was going on, but hadn't really trusted my own intuition.

"Both of us ended up crying. And both of us, I'm sure, were thinking about our wedding. Steve told me he felt he had to be honest and give me the option of calling it off. I have to admit, that did go through my mind. I was angry and sad and hurt—but at that point still absolutely sure that I wanted to get married to Steve.

"By this time, we had done two of John's seminars plus individual counseling with John. I'm sure, *sure*, that's how Steve found the strength to tell me about the affair. He had more of a sense of integrity, of self-love, of not wanting to live a lie than ever before. Seeing how honest John himself was and is about his life, seeing his high standards and sense of integrity, kind of rubbed off on Steve, I believe. I don't think he would have told me about the affair unless he had experienced these things.

"But now, after the seminars, we both had the tools to deal with this crisis. It sounds funny, but it wasn't too hard to get through it. I needed to ask a lot of questions: Where did you go? When did you sleep with her? How many times? What kind of a person was she? And we talked a lot day by day. Getting through this was a process.

"I wrote out my feelings using the love-letter format, shared them with Steve, and got his response back. And believe me, that was very,

very healing, because writing out my feelings made me very aware of the love underneath the anger and fear.

"It helped, too, to understand the overall differences between men and women. We both learned to stop giving what we wanted to receive; instead we knew how to give what the other one needed, and wanted. We understood that giving love was different for each of us, and I think that knowledge helped us to understand how it was we needed to be with each other. Without that knowledge I'm not sure we would have recovered.

> What helped me to forgive Steve completely was that I knew he had already changed.

"Another thing that helped me to forgive Steve completely was that I knew he had already changed. He had stopped seeing the woman months before, and he had new information, new tools, even a new approach to life now: he was living consciously. So I was able to trust him in what was really a pretty short amount of time, and really to forgive him. It was surprising to me that it went so smoothly, but when I think back I realize that some of it had to do with something he told me.

"He said, 'I actually thought about leaving you, Lisa, and going with her.' But he hadn't done it. He had chosen me and had stopped seeing her. That showed me that he really loved and cared about me.

"A few months later, we were married. And it was a perfect, *perfect* experience. The weather was wonderful, the setting was beautiful, we danced under the stars on a cliff above the ocean. It was an evening of perfect romance.

"Romance is still important to us; we're both very romantic by nature. But we have a two-year-old son now, and he's a very, very active Martian. So it's a little harder to have a completely romantic life, though the little things make a big difference. Steven brings me flowers a lot, and when he comes home, he finds me first before he goes to check the messages or the mail. He calls just to say hi, even when things have gotten pretty busy. Little things: reminders to me of how much he cares.

> It's so wonderful to show Donovan at such a young age these ways of interaction.

"I'm so happy to have our positive, loving communication skills, not only for us but for

Donovan, our son. Before we took John's training we yelled a lot, Steve would withdraw, and I would just panic. Here we are having a fight and he's leaving? Now we have positive, loving, open communication skills—and it's so wonderful to show Donovan at such a young age these ways of interaction.

Steve and I are both convinced that we wouldn't have the life we have today if we hadn't met John Gray—we wouldn't be married or have a child now. John rang true for us, and we learned things from him we could begin to use right away. We both feel that we are amazingly fortunate: we were open and interested and needed to know . . . and John was right there for us, just at the turning point."

Jeri and Matt

Jeri described the healing of her marriage. "On January 18, 1995, I received a phone call from an anonymous woman. She said, 'Your husband has been seeing a woman for a while and there is a child involved . . .' I hung up the phone and told my husband, who was sitting within earshot of the conversation. Initially, he denied the whole thing. Later, I lay in bed and finally blurted out, 'If there is a child involved, it can't be forgotten.'

I still hoped that the whole thing was a prank.

"My husband finally got up enough courage to say that what I had been told was true. I remember feeling sick to my stomach and racing to the bathroom. Then we went into the family room to talk. I was truly amazed at how much love I felt for this man after hearing such a horrible confession. I had always thought that if my husband ever cheated on me, our marriage would end immediately, but this was not my reaction at all.

"He told me that the affair had started three years ago and that the physical intimacy had ended one year later, when he learned that the woman was pregnant. To make matters worse, I became pregnant not long after the other woman did, so any thought of telling me then was dashed. My husband had lived with the secret that he had two sons: Patrick, our own child, and Jason, his son with the other woman. The boys were born six weeks apart. For the first year of Jason's life, my husband had barely acknowledged him, but recently Matt had been given an opportunity to reenter Jason's life. He was getting acquainted with him when I found out.

"My husband reassured me that the affair with the woman was over and that they were friends only for Jason's sake. I remember feeling surprised at his relief that I wanted him to stay, thinking to myself, Why would he think that I would want him to leave?

"In the months to come, though, I truly questioned my own thought process, for I was not reacting the way I thought a person in my position surely would. I can only attribute my acceptance of the situation to the fact that my son had a brother out there. Also, Jason was an innocent party in this nightmare and did not need to be punished. I dreamed that I could forgive my husband and that we would include Jason in our family and live happily ever after. The reality of this dream has been very hard to handle—but not because of Jason.

"Matt and I were approaching our ninth year of marriage when I found out about this situation. We had had some problems—conflicts in work and earning styles, conflicts about whether or not to buy a house, a feeling that the excitement had gone out of our relationship—and our communication was suffering. We had gone to counseling and started seeing a new counselor about six months prior to the disclosure. I was wondering if this man I loved so much had outgrown me and no longer found me enticing. Little did I know that the secret weighing so heavily on him had little to do with me!

"Shock goes along with denial. You only go through denial because the truth is too shocking to accept. For me, the denial kept away the thoughts of my husband being intimate with another woman while coming home to me. I remember thinking that this is a mistake of the past, even though the horrible picture of him with her kept popping into my mind.

"I think Matt's denial was harder for him to handle than my own was for me. He had very deep shame and was convinced that just talking about the situation wasn't good enough. He was concerned that he had ruined whatever we had and that there was so much damage it would take years to repair—if it was possible at all. Was there enough 'core love' for us to go on?

"Many times the conflicts seemed overwhelming to both of us, and there was even a time when we said we would go our separate ways. We both decided to stay, though the pain and grief was so great it seemed like a relief to be apart. I could not communicate with Matt without emotions, and he withdrew more deeply into himself. Still, we knew during this crisis that we did love each other and we were able to say so. I look back on those times and realize that we were actually communicating in a very 'Mars and Venus' fashion, trying to stay normal with work, with each other, and with our son.

Was there enough "core love" for us to go on?

"We tried many different ways of getting through this crisis. I met Jason and found that he had a sister, Jennifer, who had been abandoned by her father. I felt very strongly about protecting the children, making sure they did not get hurt and that they knew their parents' love for them was unconditional. But I was struggling too—and of course Matt was as well.

"When there is a child from an affair, the 'other woman' is still there. It's not an affair that can be forgotten easily, because the woman has to be dealt with if the child is to be seen. So my healing process was harder than normal. I often wonder about other women out there who have gone through this; I've talked with women who have experienced infidelity in their marriages, but none with children involved.

"I truly thought I was going to crack up if I didn't get away from the situation, and our therapist recommended a 'detachment,' a designated time to be apart with a promise not to make any decisions about a breakup.

"After the detachment, we took our first family vacation together, and oddly enough I sank back into a depression. It was my first time alone with Matt and Patrick in a long time, and there were no distractions. My insecurities all flooded back.

"In a kind of halfhearted way, we prepared to go back to counseling, but about a week before our scheduled visit, Matt surprised me with tickets to a John Gray seminar.

"What a seminar! It was amazing how drastically different men and women think, and throughout the room you could feel acknowledgment of that thought. I slowly began to realize that it was not a matter of how much Matt and I communicated about the problem. The important thing was understanding what was being said.

"What a relief to both of us—and apparently to others in the seminar. Many of the points Dr. Gray made that day brought a sense of relief, for he focused on how we could better understand our mates and therefore feel safe because we were not living with a stranger.

"He used humorous examples of how to ask for what you want and helped us all to realize that it was common to have 'communication problems' with your mate. The fear of asking, especially when it comes to sex, had been there for years with us. Dr. Gray was extremely graphic about what women and men want and don't want, and it helped tremendously that he had a wonderful sense of humor about it. He reassured us that both spouses in a marriage can and will make mistakes, but that relationships can get better!

"Matt and I left the seminar with a fresh awareness of each other. At this point, we already knew that we truly did love each other but that our passion was bridled with old fears. That day, I told Matt that I could put the affair behind us and that I wanted to get on with only us. And Matt surprised me with a special 'us' evening that was truly wonderful! Dr. Gray is right: the planning for 'us' evenings provides great anticipation.

"I'm not going to end this by saying 'they lived happily ever after,' because we still have hurdles to face along the way. But I can say that I now want to make Matt's and my time together a priority, and I don't feel selfish about saying this. We both know that this is just as important as raising our children.

"I thank Dr. Gray for his candor about simple areas that are not usually discussed—even among men and among women."

Julie and Larry

Julie recounted her history with Larry. "My name is Julie Anne; my husband's name is Larry. I am twenty-five years old and Larry is twenty-six. We have been married for five years and have known each other for seven. We have a five-year-old son.

"Here is our story.

"We met when I was almost nineteen and fell in love very fast. I'd been dating a boy for the past five years when we met. Larry had long hair, a loud stereo, and my parents hated him! Since they would not accept him, only four months after we met we ran off to New Mexico, where my birth mother lived (I'm adopted).

"That was all a little crazy, so we headed back to Topeka, our hometown, where we found out I was pregnant. After that, I lived with my parents and Larry with his. That was hard.

"Soon after Josh was born, Larry and I were married, and were so happy. Our only problems were money and Larry having to work so much as a car salesman. Larry decided we should move to Kansas City, saying there was more opportunity and a better place to work there. He went and I followed, but I resented him so much for taking me away from my hometown. That was when our problems began.

"Little by little, we stopped talking as much, stopped having sex as much, and stopped sharing. We hated living in the apartment we were in, and in the middle of everything we decided to buy a house. Everything really started going downhill.

"We worked hard on the house and made it beautiful, but we had a four-year-old who couldn't play outside because of the street and a wife who was lonely because her husband worked until ten every night. It was awful. We were strangers living together—roommates, I would often say.

"Then it happened. A guy I knew started giving me compliments about how pretty I was—all the things I wanted to hear from my 'roommate' but never did. I melted. It made me remember that I was not a forty-year-old trapped inside a twenty-four-year-old body.

"It was just so nice to feel young and attractive. When I talked to this man I forgot all about my home problems, which is what I should have been working on.

"I wanted a divorce. I was jealous of my divorced friends. Their lives actually started looking good to me and I really felt like I was single already!

"I just had a stranger who slept in my bed and took my covers. That was it. There just had to be something else (all the country songs fit me perfectly!).

"Meanwhile, my husband had met a woman at work. He was feeling the same scary feeling I had. This woman did the same to him as the guy had done to me—made him feel attractive again. It felt so good to him to be desired.

"When all of this came out, we were sitting in the car in Topeka. There was a lot of honesty, hand-holding, crying, and even some good ol' giggling, the way we used to do. We knew we had to start over, start over completely.

"But we got together as a team again and I started reading your books. I'd read every paragraph I could to Larry and he was very patient with me, following him around the house, reading!

"I learned such a lot from those books. I started dressing up for Larry more. And when we would get a baby-sitter, which we tried to do more often, we would go look for places to 'park.' That's fun—the excitement and risk can be very exciting. We took more showers together, and I wouldn't complain about the cold part of it and who always gets the warm water part!

There was a lot of honesty, hand-holding, crying, and even some good ol' giggling. We knew we had to start over completely.

"Larry still works some pretty long hours, but I try to keep busy with the house and my five-year-old. Then, when Larry gets home, instead of staring at the clock, I try to smile. We kiss (first thing) and we talk. Every night. We stay home more too, instead of always going out separately with friends. We feel now as if we are as one, and when we go out we are really together. That is such a nice feeling.

"We have been through quite a bit in the seven years we've known each other. It's been hard, but every part has been a lesson learned, and every day has been a new day ahead of us. I am so grateful for all that we learned and for how much we have grown in love."

Jan and David

Jan shared, "David and I have known each other since we were nine and eleven years old. At fifteen and seventeen, we began dating. Neither of us had dated anyone before that time.

"What attracted me to David was his sense of humor, friendliness, affection, and dependability. His generosity and thoughtfulness to others were important, as were his caring and concern. He got along well with my parents and family. He was fun to be around and I felt special and loved. We shared the same taste in music and enjoyed being together every chance we could get. We went steady for five years and then married in 1969.

"Over thirty years, the best time of our relationship is the happiness we have now. We are fulfilled now in ways we never thought possible during our lifetime together. The best part of our relationship is that with everything we have been through, we are still totally devoted to each other and the love didn't die.

"Also important is the fact that we were strong enough and willing enough to resolve our problems, despite the odds against us. Our emotional commitment to each other is what I consider the best part of our relationship of more than thirty years.

We are fulfilled now in ways we never thought possible during our lifetime together.

"The most consistently difficult part of our relationship has been communication. We have both had difficulty stating what we need and want from each other. This leads to resentment that can be long-term. But we have learned the importance of asking for what you want and how to tell your partner if something bothers you.

"For example, David has always preferred my hair long but never pressed the point. I preferred him without a beard but I didn't feel I could insist. When we both got what we wanted, we felt much happier. Seemingly small things can make a big difference.

"The section on communication in Dr. Gray's book *Men Are from Mars, Women Are from Venus* has helped us in our day-to-day relationship. He explains the different 'languages' of men and women and how we interpret things differently. This helped me so much in dealing with David's PTSD [post-traumatic stress disorder], which occurred after his return from Vietnam.

"David served in combat in 1969 and 1970. He did not return from Vietnam the same man I had known and married. The changes in David were so numerous I feel I can only mention the very most troublesome ones here:

- Lack of all emotions except anger, suspicion, and depression at certain times (we learned eventually that these were anniversaries of the deaths of fellow soldiers); highly critical and quick-tempered; and no more sense of humor.
- Hearing loss and tinnitus, both progressively worsening over the years.
- Bothered by helicopter noise, fireworks, parades, parties and other gatherings, war movies.

- Talked about Vietnam in conversation but refused serious discussion on the subject, and refused to admit that his war experiences had affected him.
- Needed to sit in a certain spot in a room, with his back against the wall and facing the door.
- Suffered insomnia and other sleep-related problems, especially around anniversaries of the deaths of others; slept on the living room floor off and on for thirteen years.
- Became a workaholic, but changed hobbies frequently, first obsessing then dropping them.
- Experienced emotional numbness.
- Became hypervigilant—always listening, observing; developed an exaggerated startle response.
- Had difficulty dealing with death: couldn't react to it.
- Had a need to control; always had to lead, and overreacted when someone did something "wrong."
- Had difficulty asking for what he wanted; felt he didn't deserve it.

"Needless to say, these many changes put pressure on our marriage. Three things helped us to survive them—an understanding therapist, a Vietnam veterans group, and discovering John

Gray's books and tapes. But our marriage wasn't saved and renewed until we had experienced a truly devastating situation, which almost caused us to break up.

"That experience is difficult and painful for me to think about—let alone write about—even now. About two and a half years ago, David confessed to having had a three-year affair. He had ended it, deciding he truly loved me and wanted us to be happy again. He wanted us to go to marriage counseling and finally admitted that he had problems relating to Vietnam.

"I had suspected another woman for quite some time, but repressed those feelings in my heart of hearts, because I couldn't cope with the reality—even though I had nightmares and had become physically ill from emotional stress and anxiety. When my greatest fear actually came true, I grieved for the loss of our marriage and had to decide whether to leave or stay. I had completely devoted myself to one man for my whole life and now realized that he was no longer mine alone.

"Once we entered counseling and David joined the Vietnam vet support group, we felt we needed a fresh start, a 'new marriage,' to become the partners each of us wanted. David shaved his beard and mustache and now looked like the man I had married. I grew my hair long the way he liked it. I bought David a new wedding band and had it engraved 'Love always, Jan.' Dr. Gray's books helped us through this time as well. We felt that he was writing just for us and knew our thoughts. Last year, we celebrated our twenty-fifth anniversary with a party of our family and friends.

"In conclusion, we see that we overcame our problems because we both truly wanted to be happy together and still loved each other enough to persevere through much pain, soul searching, and hard work. The effort was worth it and, as I wrote at the outset, we are happier now than when we got married.

"I would say that Dr. Gray's books helped us to see and experience each other as true soulmates; they opened our eyes to the love we always had, but that was hidden for a long, long time. Sometimes a devastating situation can be a blessing in disguise. Thank you, Dr. John Gray, from the bottom of our hearts."

Robert and Crystal

Robert talked about his own infidelities. "Crystal and I have been married for twelve years. We have three wonderful children and a beautiful home. For the first six years we had good communication and got along great. We are both successful therapists. Everything was ideal in our marriage except one thing: I started having affairs.

"Even from the beginning I was not sure that I could be monogamous, but I tried. Crystal is a beautiful woman but after a while I just lost that feeling of attraction. When we were together, I would think about other women, but at least I didn't do anything. We used to argue when I would stare at other women at the beach. She knew something was wrong but didn't know what to do. Slowly everything changed.

"Eventually I started acting on my feelings. Over a three-year period I had several affairs. I thought that if I could just fulfill my fantasies then I would become passionate for Crystal again. At first it worked, but after a while our whole relationship changed for the worse.

"I became depressed. I was helping people in their own lives but my own life was going downhill. Crystal was changing. She was no longer happy to see me; nothing I did seemed to make her happy. Everything on the outside was beautiful but on the inside we were numb.

"After reading your book, I realized that I had to tell her. It was something that I didn't seem to have any control over, and it was only hurting her to keep it from her. I told her in a letter. She was so hurt and angry. I felt so bad. But at least it was out.

"We went into counseling. She asked lots of questions about when and where. Lots of feelings were expressed. I did a lot of listening. It was a very difficult time, but she was gradually able to forgive and love me again. Her numbness lifted. Behind her feelings of anger and hurt was a beautiful, loving, and tender woman who needed my love—and I had betrayed her.

"Ironically, I had never felt so loved. Feeling sorry that I had hurt her caused me to feel again. I started feeling my attraction for her. But to fully heal and let go of her hurt and fear, my apologies, love, and attraction were not enough; she needed the reassuring message that I would never lie to her again or have an affair.

**Feeling sorry that I hurt her
caused me to feel again.**

"I didn't know what to say. How could I assure her? What if I once again lost my feelings of attraction—what would I do? My attraction for other women was still there. I could promise not to lie again, but I couldn't promise not to be attracted to other women.

"I told her that I loved her but was also still attracted to other women. It hurt her so much. Whenever we were around another beautiful woman, she would begin to close down. She knew I was attracted and I was.

"Then we watched your video seminar. When you talked about mental monogamy, it completely saved our relationship. When you said a man can love and be attracted to his wife and also be attracted to other women, we were both so relieved. You said it was normal for men to be attracted to other women but that the secret to monogamy was learning to simply direct that energy back to your partner.

"It was the easiest exercise in discipline that I have ever done. Each time I was attracted to a woman I would simply imagine making love to Crystal. It was so easy—and it works. Now I am more attracted to Crystal than ever. Being monogamous is not a jail sentence but everything I want.

"Three years later I am still doing it. If I start getting turned on by another woman, automatically I start fantasizing about my wife. I love it. I am a very visual person and now my wife is my ultimate fantasy lover. I feel like the happiest man in the world."

Nancy and Bill

Nancy told this story. "Bill and I got along very well from the start—which meant that we drank together really well. We quickly moved in together. I believe God put two drunks together to get them sober.

"Very soon, Bill was picked up for creating a disturbance while intoxicated, and I sat up all night long, thinking, thinking, wondering. Do I stay in this relationship or do I leave? What's the right thing? In the morning I went to jail to pick him up. He looked terrible.

"'What do I do?' I asked him.

"Bill didn't hesitate for a second. 'Take me to an AA meeting,' he said.

"So I did. It was our first AA meeting. Neither of us had had anything like God in our lives or any kind of higher being. But as soon as we walked in, I knew this was where we belonged, both Bill and me. All my life I had been searching for a God of understanding and a place where I knew I belonged. In AA I found those things right away.

> I believe God put two drunks together
> to get them sober.

"Six months later, Bill and I were married. We went on our honeymoon to France, where people drank from morning to night. We drank capuccino. When we got back home, we began working and eventually bought a home.

"That was when things started changing. Our marriage seemed to fall apart, and we grew away from each other. I felt as if we were just roommates—no sex, no romance, we never even saw each other.

"But there was a man at my job who seemed very understanding. I went to him and talked to him about my problems with my husband—and he told me I was beautiful, filled my head with all the things I needed to hear from my husband. One day, this man came to my house. He followed me into the bedroom where I was changing. 'It's God's will,' he told me.

"And into the bedroom walked my husband.

"When Bill saw us there together, he said the most amazing thing: 'Nancy, when you crash and burn with this man, I'll be there to pick up the pieces.'

"We didn't know what to do. Bill and I talked all night long. Was our marriage over? Should we get a divorce? Did we want a marriage that was running on empty, where we hardly saw each other and never had sex? We just didn't know what to do. I asked Bill to go with me to see a marriage counselor. Two days later I picked up *Men Are from Mars, Women Are from Venus.*

"We'd been planning a vacation, but after reading the book, I said, 'Let's change our plans and find a way to talk to Dr. John Gray. I just think he can help us.'

"'Whatever you want, Nancy,' said Bill. 'I don't want to see our marriage ending this way.'

"We went to a John Gray seminar, and just sat there with our mouths agape. Dr. Gray spoke about what I needed—what I, *Nancy,* needed—to feel loved. Just listen to me, Bill. Don't try to fix my problems. Just *be* there for me. Just listen to my day. Before that seminar, Bill would say, 'Nancy, what can I do?' Now he just listens to my day.

"And I learned to show him my appreciation for all the little things he does for me. I learned about the five things women and men need to feel loved. I learned about the huge importance of the little things—that extra hug, that extra kiss—and how to show appreciation for them.

"Everything I heard made me feel awe: it was just what both of us needed to hear to save our marriage. I had almost thrown away everything I had been looking for for almost thirty years, and here, at the seminar, I was getting it back. Both of us were.

"That weekend, Bill and I fell in love all over

again. After the seminar, we made love, and it was probably the best lovemaking session we ever had.

"The seminar changed everything for us. The best thing is that I'm just about to start a new job I really love. Before, the way I was, I didn't feel worthy of anything. But the combination of AA and John Gray's teachings helped me to love as I love right now—it's a dream come true.

"This Christmas I decided to do something really romantic for the two of us. My husband is the cook in our family, but I decided I was going to make a real Christmas dinner. I made all kinds of side dishes, I baked a ham—I had to make a lot of phone calls to get it all right, because I'd never made a dinner like that before and I didn't want to ask Bill. Then we put on a Neil Diamond album, lit candles, and sat down to dinner and to talk about our blessings.

"This Christmas we just looked at each other across the candles and experienced gratitude for everything that had happened.

"My parents' relationship was very dysfunctional, but my grandparents were together for over sixty years. I always prayed and swore that I would be like my grandmom. Every Christmas my grandmom gave me a porcelain clown, as a kind of a family tradition. This Christmas my grandmom died, but Bill gave me a present, and when I opened it, there it was: a porcelain clown. So the tradition is alive, and my grandmom's spirit is in my family. And just like my grandparents, Bill and I are going to be together until we die."

Afterword

Now, more than at any other time in history, there is a greater stress on relationships. The high rate of divorce, however, is not an indication that people are less loving, instead it indicates that people are wanting more from their relationships. In the past, men and women came together to find security. Men and women needed each other primarily to survive. Today that is not enough; now we look to each other primarily for love, happiness, and fulfillment.

Couples can grow together in love over a lifetime but it takes education and practice. There is a learning curve, and in the beginning it can be frustrating. Even with the best intentions, there will be times when we get lost and lose touch with the love in our hearts. Although we may fall out of love, with patience and the right directions, we can find it again. Like two best friends joyously finding each other after a long search, men and women can magically fall in love again and again.

I hope the stories in this book form a source of inspiration that you can return to again and again. If you have experienced emotional wounds in your relationships, these real-life stories can inspire within you a growing belief that you can heal the past and start again, willing to love and be loved. If your relationships are already strong and healthy, these stories can serve as reminders of what works. Share this book with your family and friends, talk about the stories, and search for the heart of each, where love suddenly takes on strength and begins to flourish.

In these pages we have met scores of real people inspired to put love first in their lives, to do what is necessary to preserve, protect, and cherish it, and, to keep the magic of love alive and thriving. Time and time again, these real life examples demonstrate the power of love and insight for building and rebuilding bridges in our relationships no matter what it takes. I admire the courage in these people—the courage to keep trying to make love work, the courage to remain open to new ideas and information, and the courage to assert to their partners and to the world that love is worth working for. Thank you for taking the time to make love work in your life, and thank you for letting me be a part of that process.

If you like what you just read
and want to learn more...

Call our representatives, Mars-Venus Institute, twenty-four hours a day, seven days a week, toll free, at 1-888-INFO-MVI (1-888-463-6684) or visit John Gray's website at www.marsvenus.com for information on the following subjects:

MARS-VENUS SPEAKERS BUREAU

More than 500,000 individuals and couples around the world have already benefited from John Gray's relationship seminars. We invite and encourage you to share with John this safe, insightful and healing experience. Because of the popularity of his seminars and talks, Dr. Gray has developed programs for presentations by individuals he has personally trained. These seminars are available for both the general public as well as private corporate functions. Please call for current schedules and booking information.

MARS-VENUS WORKSHOPS

The Mars-Venus Institute offers workshops that bring information to local communities around the world and trains those interested in presenting these workshops. These exciting workshops features John's favorite video segments and exercises presented by trained facilitators that have completed an in-depth course of study. Participants take home positive, practical experience that allows them to use Dr. Gray's suggestions comfortably and naturally. You can call the Mars-Venus Institute toll-free at 1-888-INFO-MVI or 1-888-463-6684. If you are out of the USA, call 415-389-6857 or look for us on our website at www.mars-venus-institute.com.

MARS & VENUS COUNSELING CENTERS

In response to the thousands of requests we have received for licensed professionals that use the Mars/Venus principles in their practice, John Gray has established the Mars & Venus Counseling Centers and Counselor Training. Participants in this program have completed a rigorous study of John's work and have demonstrated a commitment to his valuable concepts. If you are interested in a referral to a counselor in you area call 1-800-649-4155. If you seek information about training as a Mars & Venus counselor or establishing a Mars & Venus Counseling Center, please call 1-800-735-6052.

Videos, Audiotapes and Books by John Gray

For further explorations of the wonderful world of Mars and Venus, see the descriptions that follow and call us to place an order for additional information.

Mars-Venus Institute
20 Sunnyside Avenue, A-130
Mill Valley, CA 94941
1-888-INFO-MVI (1-888-463-6684)

VIDEOS

Men Are from Mars, Women Are from Venus
Twelve VHS cassettes

This is a complete collection of John Gray's work on video. In this series, Dr. Gray shares the insights and tools necessary for understanding, accepting, and loving our differences. In a positive and uplifting way, couples and singles learn to improve communication and enjoy healthy, happy relationships without sacrifice.

Mars and Venus on a Date
Seven VHS cassettes

After years of focusing on couples, Dr. Gray finally answers the thousands of singles and dating partners who asked him, "What about me?" John examines his five stages of dating: attraction, uncertainty, exclusivity, intimacy, and engagement. Find out why women need reassurance and men need encouragement. Increase your understanding of male/female differences and women's most asked question, "Why don't men commit?"

Men Are from Mars, Women Are from Venus— Children Are from Heaven

COMING SOON!

Two VHS cassettes

Dr. Gray lends his insights to parents trying to understand their little Martians and Venusians. In these cassettes you'll learn the five most important messages to give your children: It's Okay to Be Different; It's Okay to Make Mistakes; It's Okay to Have Feelings; It's Okay to Ask for What You Want; It's Okay to Say No, But Mom and Dad Are the Boss.

AUDIOTAPES

Secrets of Successful Relationships

Twelve 45-minute audiocassettes

This audio series was taped live at Dr. Gray's two-and-a-half-day seminars and features three themes: The Secrets of Communication; Getting the Love You Deserve; and The Secrets of Intimacy and Passions.

BOOKS

What You Feel, You Can Heal

An enjoyable guide to understanding and enriching your own personal growth. Learn to heal and forgive past hurts and resentments, increase your self-confidence when dealing with the opposite sex, and enjoy clear communication in a loving relationship. Dr. Gray teaches you: The Ultimate Healing Technique–The Love Letter; How to Transform the Inner Circle; How to Heal the Past; and The Power of Forgiveness.

Paperback, Heart Publishing 0-931269-01-6 $12.95

True Stories from Couples!

MARS AND VENUS IN LOVE

Inspiring and Heartfelt Stories of
Relationships That Work

Hardcover
0-06-017471-4 $18.00

Two audiocassettes
0-694-51713-5 $18.00

Keep Passion Alive!

MARS AND VENUS IN THE BEDROOM

A Guide to Lasting
Romance and Passion

Hardcover
0-06-017212-6 $24.00

Trade paperback
0-06-092793-3 $13.00

Two audiocassettes
1-55994-883-3 $18.00

Also available in Spanish:

MARTE Y VENUS EN EL DORMITORIO

Trade paperback
0-06-095180-X $11.00

Two audiocassettes
0-694-51676-7 $18.00

The Keys to Making Love Last!

MARS AND VENUS TOGETHER FOREVER

Relationship Skills for
Lasting Intimacy

Trade paperback
0-06-092661-9 $13.00

Mass market paperback
0-06-104457-1 $6.99

Also available in Spanish:

MARTE Y VENUS JUNTOS PARA SIEMPRE

Trade paperback
0-06-095236-9 $11.00

ALSO AVAILABLE:

MEN, WOMEN AND RELATIONSHIPS
Making Peace with the Opposite Sex
Mass market paperback
0-06-101070-7 $6.99
One audiocassette
0-694-51534-5 $12.00

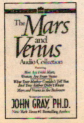

THE MARS AND VENUS AUDIO COLLECTION

Contains one of each cassette:
*Men Are from Mars, Women Are
from Venus; What Your Mother
Couldn't Tell You and Your Father
Didn't Know;* and
Mars and Venus in the Bedroom.

Three audiocassettes
0-694-51589-2 $39.00

WHAT YOU FEEL YOU CAN HEAL
A Guide for Enriching Relationships
Two audiocassettes
0-694-51613-9 $18.00